RATIONAL CHRISTIANITY

RATIONAL CHRISTIANITY

Dr. George O. Elgin

Printed in the United States of America.

ISBN: 1-59571-120-1
Library of Congress Control Number: 2006901391

Word Association Publishers
205 Fifth Avenue
Tarentum, Pennsylvania 15084

TABLE OF CONTENTS

ACKNOWLEDGEMENTS

Many people have helped to facilitate the writing of this book. Most significantly my wife, Lucy, who kept telling me, "You have good ideas. You should write a book!" Then when I started doing that, she had to put up with the many hours I spent in my "den" researching and preparing the manuscript. One of the other motivators to write this book was the encouragement of our five adult children. They grew up in a family where religion, history, medicine, philosophy and psychology were part of common family dialogues.

My adult children have not been able to find a "home church" where rationality is valued, and an organization that exudes the loving spirit of Jesus, the Christ. So I decided to write a book that would help them remember our family dialogues and pass the tradition on to our grandchildren and other friends who may be open to a rational form of Christianity as a viable option. Some of the students in various college classes I taught, also encouraged me to put my ideas into writings. Many of the participants in various church classes that I have led have also joined in encouraging me to write.

In the last chapter of this book, I have shared some of the life experiences and intellectual influences that have contributed to my approach to Christianity and life.

Some special teachers who have impacted my thought process:

During my college days, it was Professor A. Mentier, who inspired my respect for history. He made history come alive. He had minimal tolerance for irritability and stupidity. He was especially helpful to a group of student pastors who were going on to Seminary by offering us a class in the Classic Greek language.

Dr. John Howe at Wesley Theological Seminary taught that Christianity should be practical and reasonable – make a positive difference in the lives of individuals and communities. He also introduced me to the writings of Kahlil Gibran.

Dr. Herman Waetjen introduced me to a new Christology – Jesus as the Omega Human Being – while I was in my doctoral studies at San Francisco Theological Seminary. This was in a class on the gospel of John. His ideas have influenced my thinking ever since.

On the practical side, I want to thank Cheryl Roblyer for typing my handwritten, rough drafts and then redoing them after I thought of material I wanted to add, then, preparing the manuscript for publication.

My very special thanks go to Lillian Fisher, my sister in law, a retired teacher of journalism, who edited my manuscript chapter by chapter and proofread the entire document before publication. Her assistance was most helpful and deeply appreciated.

George O. Elgin
Clovis, CA

INTRODUCTION

"Never worship a God who is not at least as good and loving as you are!"

"God is the Creative Force at the heart of the Universe."
Dr. G.O. Elgin

In the war-weary republic of Vietnam in 1970 a group of American soldiers were discussing moral issues of the Vietnam War and war in general. *What actions are acceptable? What deeds are wrong, and unnecessary? What deeds are wrong, but believed by the person and viewed as necessary? How does one determine right behavior in a difficult and dangerous situation?* A Military Chaplain shared in this discussion. He asked the question, "What would God consider right behavior in this situation?" One of the senior soldiers responded, "Who the hell is God." This was more of a sarcastic remark than a sincere question. It could have been an insightful question in light of the fact that within this group were Christians, Jews and agnostics. They were living in a country where many of the people were Buddhist or Hindu. Rather than sarcasm, a more reasonable set of questions would have been: *"Whose God are we talking about? Is the God in question the only god or one of many? How do we know what the god or gods consider as moral or right behavior? Is my God actively involved in the day-to-day affairs of human lives? Can my God guide me and protect me in the midst of war?"* These are the pertinent questions that many military people ponder while serving in a combat zone. It has often been said that there are no atheists in a fox hole. While this is not totally true, it is reasonably accurate.

A badly wounded soldier was brought into the emergency room

in a military hospital in Vietnam. The nurse wanted to call a Chaplain, but did not know which Chaplain to call. The soldier was wearing a Catholic Crucifix, a Protestant Cross, and a Jewish Star of David. If he had known about the Buddha, he would probably have been wearing an image of the Buddha as well. He was trying to cover all the bases. He wanted all the protection and help he could get from whatever gods were out there. His military records revealed that he was a Baptist.

In difficult and dangerous situations, most people turn to a higher power, for all the help they can get. Carvings and drawings in ancient caves show that our earliest ancestors sought the help of, or tried to avoid the anger of Higher Powers. Some sort of religion has existed in every human society that we know about. Every major culture all over the world during the last 4000 years has had a significant religious component.

During the 20th century, the Human Family was plagued by wars, famines, economic disasters, social unrest, genocide and devastating diseases. The Cold War between the Soviet Union and the United States faced the entire human family with a real possibility of total annihilation, which poses a real challenge to their religious faith.

One current and continuing plague of the 21st century may well be terrorism. A group of radical Islamic terrorists flew hijacked commercial airplanes into the Twin World Trade Towers in New York City and the Pentagon Military headquarters in Washington DC September 11th, 2001. Well over 3000 people were killed in the aftermath. There was a surge of renewed interest in religion. One reason for this interest in religion is that this act of terror was perceived by the perpetrators as an act of religious devotion. Some conservative Christian teachers perceive the events of September 11th, 2001 as the judgment of

God. This was an expression of God's wrath, because we have allowed our society to become too secular. This is demonstrated by the fact that liberal judges have forced prayer out of the public school, powerful minority political activist groups have challenged the reference to the phrase "under God" in our Pledge of Allegiance to the flag; courts have allowed the rights of women to choose in regard to abortion; judges have declared same-sex marriage legal in the State of Massachusetts; violence and immorality pervade our movies and television programs, and pornography is a one-billion dollar a year industry in the United States. This and much more has triggered the Wrath of God. So according to some conservative Christians, God inspired these fanatic Moslem extremists to give America "A wake-up call!"

Then in December 2004, Southeast Asia was rocked by one of the most powerful earthquakes in human history. This triggered a devastating Tsunami that killed one-quarter of a million people, injuring even more people and left millions of people homeless and devastated. Radical Moslem clerics declared that this was an act of God to punish those hundreds of sinful, decadent Western tourists who were vacationing in the area. Conservative Christian clergy agreed that the disaster was the will of God.....part of God's good plan for the good of the human family.

Some rational people are asking how could a good god let all of the evil, suffering and disasters occur in this world. More people are asking a more basic question, "What good is religion?" Has the inclination toward religion enriched the human family - or has it corrupted it? Some historians believe that more people have been killed and maimed in religiously motivated wars than in all other wars combined. That is probably an exaggeration. But it does raise a question, "Has religion done more good or more harm to the people over the ages?" This causes thinking Christians to re-examine their ideas about God, and has led this author to affirm as a basic principle of rational religion, "Never worship a God who is not at least as good as you are!"

Now there are many who would say that rational religion is an oxymoron - an absolute contradiction in terms. Most religions are rooted in some sort of Divine revelation. For Jewish people God revealed the truth to Moses, which is written in the first five books of the Hebrew Scriptures, called the Books of Moses. For Christians the truth is revealed in the person of Jesus, the Hebrew Scriptures, plus the New Testament of the Bible. The New Testament is made up of books by Christians and to Christians about Jesus and how to be a Christian. In addition, Christian leaders affirm that ultimate truth is expressed in the theological statements or creeds of the Church (called orthodox) in the first four centuries of the Christian era. These would include the Apostles Creed, created at about 150 C.E. and the Nicean Creed created in 425 C.E. Mormon Christians would add the Book of Mormon, which was revealed to Joseph Smith. For members of the Islamic community, the ultimate truth is revealed in the Holy Koran revealed exactly by Allah (Arabic name for God) to the Prophet Muhammad, about 610 C.E.. These three religions are considered Religions of the Book. Their sacred scriptures are considered by most participants as the infallible directions of their God.

Following the teachings of the sacred Scriptures has motivated many people to be kind, caring, positive, and even saintly persons. On the other hand, blind obedience to various interpretations of the scriptures has contributed to murder, mayhem, war, domination and prejudice.

Human beings live their lives according to frames of reference. This is a rational frame of reference which includes education, problem-solving, science and philosophy. There is a religious frame of reference which includes devotion to or submission to a higher power or powers, and obedience to the scriptures and rules of that religion. There is a psychological frame of reference, which includes self-image, relationships, passion, emotion, pleasure and pain. There is an historical frame of reference, which includes traditional culture and respect for the past. It has been stated that those who forget the lessons of history are doomed to repeat them.

Wholesome living is a synergistic merging of information from each of the frames of reference to achieve a happy, productive and compassionate lifestyle. Rigid overcommittment to a single frame of reference is counterproductive and leads to disharmony and disease. A balanced life uses our unique ability for rational thinking, respects spirituality, cultivates positive relationships and values the lessons of history – both our personal history and the history of humanity. The following chapters will assess the negative consequences of over-commitment to the religious frame of reference and suggest a synergistic union of rationality, relationships and Christianity within an informed perspective. The goal is to develop a rationally sound, flexible religious frame of reference to guide one to fulfillment, joy, and positive relationship with other persons and with God.

PREFACE

"The unexamined life is not worth living."
Socrates

Rational Christianity is a reasonable expression of Christianity that takes seriously the disciplines of philosophy, psychology, history and theology. A plague of the early 21st century is irrationality, especially in the area of religion. Rational Christianity offers to thinking people an option to be truly Christian without accepting absolutism in regard to the creeds or the Bible. The doctrines of the church are considered within an historical prospect; they are examined for logical consistency, and the positive or negative impact on members of the human family are considered. Rational Christians acknowledge their humanness – they do not have absolute truth. What they do have is a God worthy of worship and the freedom to subject traditional Christianity to rational analysis.

Aristotle, the Greek philosopher, maintained that rationality is the key feature that distinguishes human beings from other animals. In this book, rationality is contrasted with irrationality.

Beliefs that are contrary to the dictates of reason are irrational. Among rational beings some beliefs are non-rational since they are matters of taste and no reasons are required. These are beliefs that just don't matter significantly. However, irrational beliefs can be dangerous and destructive.

Reason is the general human faculty or capacity for truth-seeking and problem-solving as contrasted with instinct, imagination or faith, in that rational conclusions are intellectually trustworthy.

Theology and philosophy have important overlapping concerns. Both address the matters of ethics, human freedom, and the quest for truth. Philosophy is a human effort to discover wisdom – a consistent frame of reference that defines the nature of reality and the proper behavior of human beings in order to achieve personal happiness and contribute to the welfare of the human family. A philosophy that fails to address the existence of God or gods and the issue of continued existence after death is seriously incomplete according to The Oxford Companion to Philosophy.

Theology is usually based on truth revealed by some divine source. Systematic theology presents a frame of reference, a paradigm that explains the nature of the universe, how human beings relate to the creative force of the universe in order to have happy productive lives, and the expectation of a continued positive existence after death. Any theology that offers mixed messages about the nature of the Creative Force, that has blatant internal inconsistencies and tries to defend these inconsistencies by calling them paradoxical truth or as divine mysterious, is seriously flawed.

From the earliest days of my childhood, until the present, it has been my naive understanding that to be a Christian meant to be a person who modeled their life according to the example and teachings of Jesus. In Sunday School and at home, I learned about the life of Jesus. I learned the simplest of his teachings, like the Beatitudes at the beginning of the Sermon on the Mount, the Golden Rule – do unto others what you would want others to do, and Jesus loves you.

During my childhood, I began to have questions about this early understanding of Christianity. I observed a lot of people who claimed to be Christians who clearly did not model their behavior after the example of Jesus and seemed unaware of the simplest of his teachings.

I remember as a very young person over hearing adults discussing a book called In His Steps, written by Charles M. Sheldon, a Congregational minister. I understood that a group of Christians – a church or some religious community – had made a commitment to check their daily behavior by the challenge, "What would Jesus do?" They agreed to do this for some specific period of time. What I overheard was how radical this action was and what amazing changes occurred in their lives as a result. I was confused by this discussion because I thought that this was the behavior expected from every person who claimed to be Christian.

As I became more cognizant of human behavior around me, I began to realize that a lot of Christians did not seem to let the example and teachings of Jesus interfere with the way they chose to live. The amazing discovery to me was that some of those people who claimed to be most pious – most correctly Christian – were very mean, judgmental and arrogant. They did not even seem to be very happy. Their greatest joy was the "knowledge" that their practice of Christianity was the only "correct" way to be Christian. All other groups who claimed to be Christian, at best, were wrong and at worse were evil.

This behavior was most obvious among the people in the extremely fundamentalist holiness churches my family attended when possible. As I began to try to understand the teachings of these churches, I learned that the first step in being a Christian was to accept Jesus as your Savior and ask God to forgive your sins through Jesus. This was the experience they called "being saved." If you were going to be truly Christian, you needed a second work of grace - to be "sanctified" – that is God would come into your being, remove the genetic flaw of original sin and take full control of your life so that every thing you did would be directed by the Holy Spirit and reflect the example of Jesus. This was a Biblical belief system based on the teachings of Saint Paul in the New Testament. The only problem I found with this theory, as a young person, is that I never met a person who demonstrated the theory in practice. I saw lots of people who claimed to be "filled by the Holy Spirit" or "sanctified," whatever term you use, but they were still mean, critical, arrogant, and not very much like the Jesus I had learned about.

Reflecting back on those years, I now know that I was experiencing cognitive dissonance.

Cognitive dissonance is a psychological term for the inner stress caused when clearly affirmed ideas or values are incongruent with the reality of human behavior. This term is used in sociology when affirmed organizational values conflict with the actual behavior of leaders or organization. A modern example of this can be seen when President George Bush first ran on a unity platform. He was going to unite the American people and lead them in a bipartisan manner. The reality that followed his election is that the country became increasingly divided and hostility between the political parties increased significantly. This is COGNITIVE DISSONANCE!

In my religious experiences as a teenager, I experienced the stress of cognitive dissonance because the doctrines of the church did not match up with my observation of human behavior.

One way to mitigate the stress of cognitive dissonance is to revise the belief system to eliminate unrealistic expectations.

A new and different experience of Christianity took place when I served a three-year enlistment in the U.S. Army. The last two years, I was assigned to a somewhat remote military installation in Germany. Soon after being assigned to that base I started meeting with a group of other young men on a weekly basis for Bible study. This was a transformational experience for me. In this group, I discovered people from various religious backgrounds – Methodists, Baptists, Presbyterians – who could discuss their beliefs without insisting that their way of understanding the Bible was the only right way. The focus was on modeling our lives by the example and teachings of Jesus. This was a warm, accepting, supportive Community of Faith.

This experience launched me on a life journey to develop a model of Christianity in which the ideals of the Faith could be realistically achieved by individuals and organizations for the good of the whole human family.

With that experience of Christian Community, I began to examine traditional expressions of Christianity by the importance they give the life and teachings of Jesus, and how diligent are these Christians in practicing the religion of Jesus.

After my experience in the military, I married my wife Lucy and she joined me in the intellectual/spiritual quest to discover a form of Christianity that was positively pragmatic and intellectually honest. My professional training in college and two seminaries equipped me more fully in this quest. Lucy and I were fortunate to have five great children. In our family life the subjects of religion, philosophy and psychology were frequently discussed. Years of pastoral experience, and service as an Army chaplain all fueled my desire to offer an expression of Christianity which focused on the life and teachings of Jesus, and provide a God worthy of worship – a positive faith that would equip people to make the most of this life, and not worry about end times, and not focus too much attention on life after death.

After our children became adults, I realized that our family discussions had been helpful to them. Lucy and the children encouraged me to put my ideas on paper. This is how this form of Rational Christianity was written as a guide for pragmatic, thinking people – who desire to make this world a better, kinder and more peaceful place.

Chapter I
Does Religion Matter?

"Science without religion is lame,
religion without science is blind."
Albert Einstein

CLEARLY RELIGION HAS A SIGNIFICANT IMPACT ON THE behavior of people in human society. It can be a motivation for very positive and constructive behaviors. And it can be a motivation for hatred or conflict and all kinds of negative consequences. The power of religion is clear, when we examine the history of those societies that tried to eliminate religion. In almost every case, they failed. Human beings seem to be naturally, intuitively, inclined to be religious. Anthropologists define religion in this way: Religion is everywhere an expression of one form or another of a sense of dependence on a power outside ourselves, a power, which we may speak of as spiritual or moral power.

In the earliest human societies, religion became associated with survival. The society was confronted by natural realities that were beyond their control such as the need to find food in hunting and gathering societies. People in these societies came to believe that there was a higher power or powers. Witch doctors or priests were the members of the society that could contact these higher powers. They developed the rituals and rules that would facilitate successful survival. The earliest example of possible religious activity among our earliest ancestors was about 10,000 B.C. It was probably a form of sympathetic magic. They painted pictures of successful hunts on the walls of their caves or they made clay models of the animals that were being hunted, and destroyed them by throwing objects at them. This was probably done while the hunters were out in the field seeking game. These people were called Cro-Magnon people because their paintings and other artifacts were found in the Cro-Magnon Cave in southern France.

The logical question is did these religious efforts make a real difference in the physical world? The truth is that there is no way of knowing. It is clear that early societies believed that these religious rituals did make a difference. Or they would not have continued to practice. The fact is that perception is reality for the perceiver. Perceiving that they could influence higher powers motivated them to increase their efforts and thus stimulated their evolutionary progress of social development.

Religion as an institution, developed when hunting and gathering people became more settled into agricultural communities. This happened at various times in different locations in our world. One of the earliest of this type of community is dated to about 7500 B.C. in the Jordan River Valley. Similar agricultural cultures appear in Egypt and Mesopotamia about 5000 B.C. A religious ritual common to most of these cultures was the rain-making ritual. The community would gather as a group, while the religious leader would pour water over samples of their crops, accompanied by prayers and sometimes by the sacrifice of either human being or an animal. As societies achieved the domestication of animals and greater cultivation of crops in these agricultural communities, the worship of fertility gods developed. Rituals to encourage the gods to help the herds be fertile, and the crops be plentiful, were practiced. Rules of behavior that would avoid making the gods angry were established. When disasters occurred the gods were angry and had to be appeased. Often human sacrifice was used to satisfy the angry god. As cultures became more civilized, they transitioned from human sacrifice to animal sacrifice.

The question, "Does religion matter?" on an individual level depends on one's status in society. In these early societies, it mattered to the Kings or Chiefs, because they often claimed to be the representative of, or incarnations of, the greatest local god, and as such had absolute power within the society. As a result, in ancient Egypt and many of the Mesopotamian cultures, the priests became an elite social class, second in power only to the King. Religion was the source of their status and power.

If one was among the lowest status in the culture, religion mattered even more! During a greater part of the Shang Dynasty in China, 1766 to 1123 B.C., human sacrifice was practiced on a large scale. The victims were those taken in battle. If they ran out of victims, raiding expeditions were sent out to get more victims for sacrifice. The Canaanite religion in the Jordan River valley in the period 1300 to 900 B.C. practiced human sacrifice and Temple prostitution. The conflict between Hebrew religion and Canaanite religion is a subject of interest in the Hebrew Scriptures. Again, the victims were those of the lowest status in society. In the religions of the Americas and the 10th to 15th centuries of this Current Era, human sacrifice was very common. In the Aztec Empire human sacrifice was a major part of the religion. Again, the victims were mostly prisoners of war or slaves. When they ran out of prisoners, they launched a new campaign to get a good supply of victims for human sacrifice. Clearly, religion mattered as an instrument of power and status for people at the top of the hierarchy, and religion mattered even more as a life or death issue for those in the lowest and most vulnerable members of the societies.

Religion mattered significantly to witches. True witches practice a ritualistic religion that is somewhat secretive. Witches are viewed as suspicious or dangerous by the major religions of any society. In several ancient societies, people who were thought to be witches were summarily executed by order of the religious authority. This practice was continued into relatively modern time. In 1484, Pope Innocent VIII ordered Papal Inquisitors to root out all witchcraft, using whatever drastic means were available. That usually meant burning them at the stake. In the 1500's, in Geneva, Switzerland under the Protestant leader John Calvin, witches were also executed. In the Protestant and Catholic countries in Europe in the late 15th and 16th Centuries, there was an unexplained hysteria about witches. Literally thousands of old women and young girls, even children, were tortured and killed in the name of religion. Witches were thought to be the cause of natural disasters, and epidemics. Even in colonial America there were witch trials in Salem. To true witches, religion did matter because it was their way to understand the higher powers. Religion mattered even more to those innocent people accused of being witches because accusation could mean torture or death.

In the case of those persons who dared to challenge the established religion of their community, religion mattered significantly. For example, Socrates was accused of corrupting the morals of the youth of Athens by his philosophical questionings. He was sentenced to death by the people of Athens in the year 495 B.C. The same may be said for Jesus of Nazareth. He was accused of blaspheming God by claiming to be the Son of God. This led to his execution by the Romans on a cross about 27 or 28 C.E. John the Baptist, a contemporary of Jesus, was executed by King Herod for criticizing the failure of the king to obey the religious rules of that society. Many Christians in the first three centuries of this Current Era were tortured or executed for refusing to honor the Roman Emperor as a God. This is another example of religion working well for those in power positions, and not very well for people in lesser positions in society.

Christianity became a legal religion in the early 4th Century when the Emperor Constantine became a Christian. Some years later Christianity became the official religion of the Roman Empire. The Emperor Constantine directed the Christian Bishops of the entire empire to meet for a Church Council at the city of Nicea in order to define the true beliefs of the Christian faith. The results of that Council is known as The Nicean Creed. Christians who accepted this Creed were known as Orthodox Christians. Orthodox Christianity means Christianity as practiced by the Christians in Rome. Orthodox Christianity claimed to be the only correct understanding of the Faith and claimed that this was the exact teaching of the Apostles and Jesus himself. Those Christians who did not accept Orthodox Christianity were considered to be heretics and often were excluded from the Christian community. Later in Christian history, these heretics were executed for their improper beliefs. This practice continued until after the Protestant Reformation in the 16th Century. Religion clearly mattered for those free-thinking persons within a Christian community and did not accept the Orthodox views of Christianity.

Other historic events that demonstrate that religion matters include The Crusades which were military ventures ordered by the Pope in Rome to save the Holy Lands from the Moslems. The Crusades were motivated by religion, but the victims were often the unfortunate people who happened to be in the path of the Crusaders. Another example of an historical event where religion triggered war was in Germany from 1618 until 1648, a period known as the Thirty Years War. The Catholic King of Austria and other Catholic leaders in Southern Germany were determined to force the people of northern Germany to give up their Protestant Christian beliefs and return to proper Catholic belief. Over the thirty years, thousands of people died and more were injured; a lot of property was destroyed. Neighboring nations got involved but at the end, things were just about the same as when the war began. Religion mattered as an excuse for the war. The real reasons probably had more to do with power and economics.

Religion mattered to the separatist religious groups in the 17th Century in England. They chose not to practice the religion of The Church of England. One group sought freedom in the new world and established the Plymouth Colony in America. Here they were free to practice THEIR religion. People who had different religious beliefs were expelled and formed their own colonies. When the thirteen American Colonies rebelled against England and established The United States of America, true religious freedom became a basic principle of the country.

Does religion matter in the 21st century? Consider the country of Afghanistan, beginning in the 1990's, a group of radical fundamentalist Islamic clerics took control of the government. They established an Islamic state in which Islamic law interpreted by their group of fanatical clergy was imposed on all the citizens. All phases of public life were dictated by religious authority from the clothes women could wear to the length of men's hair and their beards. Religious police patrolled the streets and all dissenters were harshly punished. The leaders of Afghanistan opened their country to other religious fanatics like Osama Bin Laden, and his Al Qaeda revolutionary group. They proclaimed holy war on all infidels and especially on Americans. They established training camps for terrorists in order to teach them how to destroy and kill in the name of Allah. Thousands of fanatics from all over the world came for that training. The events of September 11th, 2001, when 20 of these fanatic terrorists hijacked commercial airlines in the United States and flew them into the World Trade Towers in New York City and the Pentagon in Washington, DC. were an expression of that holy war. The suicidal fanatics were performing an act of extreme devotion to their God. This is a modern form of the old practice of human sacrifice, which has haunted religious people for centuries. The immediate effect of the events of September 11th, 2001, led the United States to launch a war on terrorism and the first action was to replace the government of Afghanistan, to destroy their training centers for terrorists, and to restructure their society.

Also, during the 1990's into early 2000, the conflict between the nation of Israel and the Palestinian people was almost impossible to resolve because of religious fanaticism. There were fanatics on both sides, but the most serious fanatics were the suicide bombers and were encouraged by Islamic clerics to strap explosives to their bodies and to go into Israel and blow themselves up in places where they could kill a significant number of Israeli people. The people recruited for this task were not the rich and well-educated. As usual their recruits were the poor, unemployed and hopeless members of that society. They were encouraged by their religious leaders to serve God by killing Jews. These poor victims of ridiculous fanatical religion were promised great rewards in the afterlife for being martyrs for their faith. It is most unfortunate that these religious leaders did not lead by examples as this would rid society of destructive fanatics. This is another example of human sacrifice in the name of religion perpetrated by educated leaders on gullible, vulnerable poor people within the society.

From our earliest beginnings as human beings until the present, religion really **does** matter. It has been used by the highest levels of society to support their positions of power and authority. Religion has been used to control, manipulate and intimidate the common folk. For the least, the marginalized and the most vulnerable, religion has been justification for isolation, persecution and even executions. On the positive side, religion has inspired many people at all levels of society to greatness in service, compassion and the pursuit of peace with justice for all. It has been a significant source of courage and consolation in times of tragedy and loss. For good or for ill, religion DOES matter in people's lives.

(Primary Source for historical information about religions in this chapter: World Civilizations, Vol. I and II; Burns, Ralph, Lerner, & Meacham 7th Edition; W.W. Norton & Company, N.Y., 1986)

Chapter II

Impact of Theology on People

"As he thinketh in his heart, so is he."

Proverbs 23:7 (KJV)

IT IS CLEAR THAT RELIGION HAS A SIGNIFICANT IMPACT ON human societies; some are very positive and some very negative. This chapter will focus on the impact of Theology on people. Within almost all religions, there is a God concept, an understanding of the nature of Supreme Beings, Gods, Goddesses or a God. Since these are perceived as supreme beings, people's beliefs about their God or gods has a significant impact on their attitudes and behavior.

This chapter will focus on those major religions which are monotheistic, theoretically having only one God. These would be Judaism, Islam, and Christianity. Our primary focus will be on Christianity. There are some parallels in Islam and Judaism.

Beliefs about God begin in childhood from the teaching and religious practice of parent figures. If the family is actively involved in their religion, children will receive instruction from organized religious institutions. These teachings are generally presented as absolute truths, not subject to question. As children advance in education and maturity toward adulthood, they often begin to re-examine and even challenge the absolutes they have been taught. Their theology evolves based on their experience and their appreciation of history. Unfortunately, many people are taught to place the absolute of religion in a mental lock box, never to be challenged or changed. These may be brilliant, well-educated people with inquiring minds who are very open to new ideas in most areas, but not religion. The absolutes of religion must be accepted as ultimate truth. The absolute authorities may be the Church, the Scriptures or the particular community of Faith in which they are involved. The God Concept that people accept or develop has a direct effect on their image of themselves and their relationship with other people. It is not clear whether people behave like the God they believe in or if their God is the projection of their own personality. If people are willing to engage in a dialogue about Theology, their description of God may be a clue to their approach to life. If they describe a righteous God who hates sin and is angry with sinners, they may well be people who have unreasonable expectations of other people and get angry when people do not live up to them. If there is a strong focus on "end times" and final judgment, such believers may be very judgmental people themselves. People who describe their God as a loving and forgiving God may themselves be more loving and forgiving than most people. At best, people's description of their God may be only a clue to their behavior. However, those people who have their religion secured in a mental lock box, may not let religion overly influence their personal behavior.

A person's Theology may contribute a strong component to their self-image. For Christians, the Bible offers two uniquely different strains of thought about who we are as human beings.

The positive view of who we are as human beings begin in the first chapter of Genesis, the first book of the Bible. This is the story of God creating the universe in seven celestial days. At the end of each creative day, God surveys the work and pronounces it as good. On the sixth day God said, "And now we will make human beings; they will be like us and resemble us…" So God created human beings, making them to be like himself. He created them male and female. "God looked at everything that he had made, and he was very pleased." (Genesis 1: 26-31a NEV) When people read this passage carefully, they often ask who is God addressing when he says, "Now we will make human beings." Who is the "we"? There are many scholarly speculations about this, but there is not complete agreement. In the book of Proverbs, there is an interesting possibility. Wisdom is calling out to the human family. She says, "Listen to my excellent words; all I tell you is right. What I say is the truth; lies are hateful to me….(v-8) The Lord created me first of all, the first of his works, long ago. I was made in the very beginning, at the first before the world began (verses 22, 23)….. I was beside him like an architect, I was his daily source of joy, always happy in his presence – happy with the world and pleased with the human race." (Verses 30, 3 1) (Proverbs 8 NEV) Human beings were created by the power of love at the heart of the universe. Love creates Wisdom, and in joyous activity creates the world and human beings. Human beings are good and like God; they have self-awareness, freedom of choice and the potential for loving. To whatever degree they exercise the potential of loving, they participate in the joyous life of the Divine.

This very positive view of human beings is present in the eighth Psalm where the Psalmist says," O Lord, our Lord, your greatness is seen in all the world!... When I look at the sky, which you have made, at the moon and the stars which you set in their place – what is man that you think of him; mere man that you care for him? Yet you made him inferior only to yourself, you crowned him with glory and honor. You appointed him ruler over everything you made." Ps. 8:1, 3-6a NEV). One of the other translations words it differently, indicating human beings as little less than God. So in the first chapter of the first book of the Bible, in the Psalms and in the Proverbs, we learn that human beings are made in the image of God, little less than God, and a very good and powerful element in God's Creation.

This positive theme is expressed in the gospels of the New Testament where Jesus teaches that God is a loving Father who loves every one of his children and invites them into an intimate relationship with Him. In the opening chapter of the Fourth Gospel is a passage very similar to the passage in Proverbs. A loose translation of the opening words of John's gospel is "In the beginning was the Word." The Word was moving toward God. (Moving towards intimacy is the positive action of love.) The word became one with God and love exploded into Creative activity. The Greek word translated as "word" is Logos and could also be translated wisdom or reason. In verse 14, the writer says that the Word became a human being and lived among us. This is called the Incarnation. Jesus in love moved toward God and God moved toward him and they became one in the intimacy of Love. What Jesus taught his disciples is that every human being who exercises his potential for loving by loving God, loving his neighbor, and truly loving himself could achieve a degree of oneness with God and participate in the life of the Divine. Jesus said that whoever believes his message and walks in his way has eternal life – may currently participate in the life of the Divine.

This may be what the great Christian evangelist Paul meant when he wrote to the Ephesian Church and said, "I, therefore, the prisoner of the Lord, beseech you to walk worthy of the calling with which you were called, with all gentleness, with long suffering, bearing with one another in love .... There is one body, and one Spirit, just as you were called in one hope of your calling, one Lord, one faith, one baptism, one God and Father of all, who is above all, and through all and in you all." Eph. 4:1-6 (NKJV)

Later in the same letter, Paul says, "Since you are God's dear children, you must try to be like him. Your life must be controlled by love, just as Christ loved us." (Eph. 5:1,2a (NEV))

The love connection between human beings and God is described even more clearly in the first Epistle of John. "Dear friends, let us love one another, because love comes from God. Whoever loves is a child of God and knows God. Whoever does not love does not know God, for God is Love.... No one has ever seen God, but if we love one another, God lives in union with us, and his love is perfected in us." (I John 5:7,8,12 NEV)

As Christians we can appropriate these positive affirmations to our own self-image. We are made in the image of God, created by Love to be loving persons. We are loved by the Creator and invited into an intimate relationship of oneness with God. The extent to which that oneness is realized depends on our exercising our potential for loving by loving God, loving other people and properly valuing ourselves.

The negative themes concerning human beings also begins in the Book of Genesis in Chapter 2, Verse 4. This is the second story of creation. This mythological story of creation is older than the first story. It was probably told around camp fires and at family gatherings for over a thousand years before it was written down in the Book of Genesis. If this story is read as a creation myth, there are a number of lessons to be learned about human nature. If it is read as a literal description of the way things got started, the result is bad theology and inadequate science. If taken too seriously, this story is loaded with negative ideas about human beings. The first is about the role of women. First God made man from the dust of the earth and breathed into his nostrils the breath of life and he became a living soul. Interesting to note that man was just a dirt model until he could breathe on his own.

Then he became a living soul. God knew that it was not good for man to be alone so God created a bunch of animal friends for Adam. These friends did not really satisfy Adam's need for community. So God made a woman out of one of Adam's ribs. Adam was pleased with God's new creation. It is important that Woman was made to be Adam's helper, not his equal partner. Eve was tempted by the Serpent to eat fruit from the forbidden tree with the promise that it would make her equal with God. Adam must have wanted to be equal with God also or maybe he was afraid of being inferior to Eve. He ate the fruit also. "As soon as they had eaten, they were given understanding and realized that they were naked; so they sewed fig leaves together to cover themselves. (Genesis 3:7 NEV) Now they understood that it was shameful to be naked. They were now thinking like God for when they encountered God, he sewed animal skins together to cover their nakedness. This idea that the naked human body is somehow a shameful thing to see is still with us. Many people are ashamed of their bodies.

When God questioned Adam and Eve about why they had broken his rules, we are introduced to the "blame game." They blamed God for their failure. Adam says "that woman you put here with me gave me the fruit and I ate it." (Genesis 31 NEV) When God questioned the woman, she answered that the snake God had created had deceived her. God did not give the snake a chance to make excuses. He punished the snake condemning him to crawl on his belly. God punished the woman by giving her pain in childbirth and by making her SUBJECT to her husband. The man was punished by God, cursing the earth and causing weeds to grow so that man would have to work hard and sweat to produce the food he needed to survive." The Lord God said, "Now that the man has become one like us and has knowledge of what is good and what is bad, he must not be allowed to eat fruit from the tree of life, and live forever."

(Genesis 3:22 NEV) So God kicked them out of the Garden and placed an angel with a flaming sword at the only entrance to make sure that they did not get to the tree of life. God told Adam that since he had come from the dust of the earth, when he died, he would return to the dust of the earth. God told Eve that because she ate the forbidden fruit, she would have pain in childbirth and that she would forever have her husband rule over her. God told Adam that because he had been disobedient, God would curse the earth causing weeds and thorns to grow so that Adam would have to work hard to get food from the earth.

This second creation story begins many negative themes about the Human family which will recur frequently in the Bible. First, man is made of dust and at death, returns to dust. There is no concept of another life in another place. The end is the end. The Book of Ecclesiastes picks up on this theme. For the writer of Ecclesiastes, this life is all there is, so make the most of it while you have it, because when it's over – it's over. In Jesus' time, this was the belief of the Sadducees. They challenged Jesus about the belief in resurrection or life after death. Their challenge is found in Luke 20:27-40.

The most obvious and persistent negative theme is about the role of women. Eve was made as an after-thought by God to be a "helper" for Adam. As they are being expelled from the Garden of Eden, God specifically says that the woman is to be subject to the man. This theme is spoken and acted out in most of the Old Testament. It is stated emphatically in the letters attributed to Paul in the New Testament. Paul says to the church at Corinth that man "reflects the image and glory of God. But woman reflects the glory of man, for man was not created for woman, but woman for man. Nor was man created for woman's sake, but woman was created for man's sake." (I Cor. 11:7-9) Note the power of this ancient creation myth. It was dictated the role of women for three or four thousand years in Judaism, Islam and Christianity. This idea of male superiority is still being preached from Christian pulpits. The Roman Catholic church will not permit women to be priests. Many conservative Christian churches will not let women have high offices in the church.

The important negative theme of sin, known in Christianity as the Doctrine of Original Sin, has its origin in the Adam and Eve narrative. If the Serpent in this story had been truly wise, he would have told Eve to first eat fruit from the Tree of Life before eating from the Tree of Knowledge of Good and Evil. When Adam and Eve ate the forbidden fruit, sin was born into the world. Sin then became a genetic flaw in all future human beings. In Psalm 51:5, the Psalmist says, "Behold, I was brought forth in iniquity, and in sin did my mother conceive me." (Ps. 51:5 NKJV). In another modern translation that reads "I have been evil from the time I was born; from the day of my birth, I have been sinful." (Ps. 51:5 NEV) This is why many Christian churches insist on a baby being baptized as soon as possible. The Sacrament of Baptism will allow God to forgive the child for the sin of being human. Paul, writing in this letter to the Romans, quotes from Psalm 14 these words, "There is no one who is righteous, no one who is wise or who worships God. They have turned away from God; they have all gone wrong; no one does what is right, not even one." (Rom. 3:10-12 NEV) What a negative image of the human family. It is interesting that these totally negative views of the human family are absent from the teachings of Jesus.

The Bible offers two distinctively different views of who we are as humans. The positive view sees us as made in the image of God - little less than God - partners with God in the creative activity of loving. The negative view sees us as inherently evil - unable to do anything good - totally dependent on God's grace to choose some people for salvation and to torture the rest in the fires of Hell.

Unfortunately, the negative themes of the Bible have received more attention in Christianity than the positive themes. The choice of the positive or the negative theme is made based on one's Theology, or God concept. The God concept one choose to accept will consciously or unconsciously influence one's self-image and one's relations with other people.

People who believe that every word in the Bible is the exact words of God, are trapped by theology. They have to try to reconcile the God of the Old Testament, the God described by Paul, or the God of Jesus described in the Gospels. When it comes to ethical behavior they tend to use quotations from the Bible to justify their actions. Using the Bible in this way can justify all kinds of negative behavior. If people are jealous, they can quote the Ten Commandments where God is reported as saying: "For I, the Lord your God am a jealous God." God destroys those who reject him and blesses all who keep his commandments. If God is jealous and demands loyalty and obedience, then I can be jealous and demand loyalty and obedience from my wife, or husband, and my children. In two places the Bible directs "an eye for an eye and a tooth for a tooth." (Exodus 21:24 and Leviticus 24:20). Since God loves those who love him and punishes those who are unfaithful and rebellious, why should we not do the same. Those who choose to behave in this way have Biblical support but they choose to ignore the clear teachings of Jesus in this matter.

For many Christians, God is the all-seeing eye, observing and recording all of our deeds and even our thoughts in order to judge us according to our deeds. The writer of the Proverbs says, "God knows and judges your motives. He keeps watch on you; he knows, and he will reward you according to what you do." (Proverbs 24:27 NEV) In his letter to the Romans, Paul says, "God will reward every person according to what he has done .... For God judges everyone by the same standard (Romans 2: :6,11). For those people whose theology focuses on the righteousness of God and his utter disdain for sin and evil doers, life can became a frightening experience. They know that they have done evil things and had evil thoughts. They live in fear of the day when they have done enough evil things to trigger the anger of God. This underlying fear is evident when parents experience one of their children dying. Their questions are: *Why did God do this to me? What did I do wrong to deserve this?* This comes from a theology that over-emphasizes the righteousness of God and the wrath of God. Some people who share this understanding of God, on a conscious or an unconscious level, assume that if God can be demanding and acting out in anger, it is legitimate for them to act in the same way.

Another negative theological theme that permeates the Bible, especially in the Old Testament, is the nature of God's love for humanity. One of the significant teachings of Jesus was that God loved every one of his children, the rich and the poor, the powerful and the marginalized, the good and the bad. God's love according to Jesus is unconditional and universal. This is not the primary theme of the Old Testament and some of the New Testament. The prominent image of God is that he only loves who worship him properly and behave in the way that pleases him. Look at the story of Noah in Chapters 6-8 in Genesis. God looked at the human family and decided that they are all evil and have evil thoughts. The only real evil described is violence. The writer of Matthew's Gospel in his long essay on end-times (Ch. 24) likens it to the days of Noah. He identifies the sins of the people before the flood. "In the days before the flood people ate and drank, men and women married, up to the very day that

Noah went into the boat." God regretted that he made human beings and decided to terminate them except for Noah who worshipped him properly. So the great and holy just God of the universe perpetuated the first genocide in the human family. If the people's violence was evil, how much more evil is the catastrophic violence of God?

In Paul's letter to the Romans he defends God's action (Romans 9:18-23). Since God made human beings he can do anything he wants with them. He has made some to be objects of his mercy and all the rest he made to be objects of his wrath. (Just for the fun of it!) The God of the Old Testament had a genocidal propensity. When the people of Israel were ready to occupy the Promised Land, God's instructions were clear. (Deut. 20:16-18) They were ordered to kill everyone in the cities they captured. Don't cut down the fruit trees, but kill all the people. In I Samuel 15, God gave orders to King Saul, the first King of Israel, to attack the Amalekites, a kingdom south of Israel and destroy them. Kill every man, woman, child and baby and kill all of the cattle and sheep. Because Saul did not do this completely, God deserted him as King. This God is not a god whose love is somewhat conditional. He is pure and simple – a genocidal maniac.

When we examine God's relationship with the people of Israel, there is a God who is conditional. From the time of the giving of the law at Mt. Sinai throughout the ancient history of the nation of Israel, God's love is clearly conditional. If they obey his laws and worship him properly, God will bless them. If they disobey his laws or do not worship him properly, he will destroy them.

Some of these stories may be mythological, and the rest may be history with a theological "spin." The image of God in this material is a God whose love is highly conditional. This is in sharp contrast to the teachings of Jesus who describes a God who loves unconditionally. The life of Jesus is a demonstration of unconditional love.

People who believe strongly in a God whose love is conditional will very probably practice conditional love in their relationships. People who accept the teaching and example of Jesus that God's love is unconditional will endeavor to love people unconditionally. If the creative energy at the heart of the Universe is unconditional love, the more we learn to love in this manner, the more we are in harmony with God.

Chapter III
Questioning Traditional Beliefs About God

*"Believe those who are seeking truth;
doubt those who have found it."*

Andre Gide

"God is subtle but he is not malicious."

Albert Einstein

IN SUNDAY SCHOOL CLASSES, IN CHRISTIAN SCHOOLS, AND in pulpits around the world the omnipotence of God is emphatically proclaimed. But thinking people are beginning to wonder about that claim. One woman asked her pastor recently, "If God is all powerful, why would he let a man like Hitler murder millions of innocent people? Why didn't he stop him?" For centuries people have asked, "If God is all powerful, why does he let the innocent suffer?" Why does God permit earthquakes to kill and injure thousands of people in an instant of time?

If God is, in fact, all powerful, then he is totally responsible for all the evil and all of the tragedy of the world. The question of an anguished mother when informed that her son has been killed in action in Vietnam, "Why did God do this to me?" is justified. If God is all powerful, he did kill her son!

According to my theological framework (working hypothesis),

God is not all powerful. His power is severely limited in several areas. These limitations may be self-imposed but they are none the less real. There are many things which God can not and will not do.

First, God is limited by his nature. He can not do anything that conflicts with his basic nature. Jesus said, "For a good tree bringeth forth good fruit, neither doth a corrupt tree bring forth good fruit . . . a good man out of the good treasure of his heart bringeth forth that which is good; and an evil man out of the evil treasure of his heart bringeth forth that which is evil." If this is true of men, that they reflect their true nature in their deeds, how much more true it is of God. If God is good and his true nature is love, then it is impossible for him to do anything that contradicts that nature.

It is, therefore, impossible for God to be jealous. Jealousy is born in selfishness and is sustained on hatred. Jealousy is a vice totally unworthy of a loving God. A deity who can be provoked to jealousy (I Kings 14:22 or Deuteronomy 32:16) can not be good and loving also. Jealousy and true love are contradictory emotions. Jealousy conflicts with the basic nature of God. The ancient Hebrew God was the God of their nation only, became consumed with anger, changed his mind frequently, and in general, possessed many frailties common to man. A broader, higher concept of God as the loving, dependable Father of all people demands that many deeds once explained as acts of God can be explained in a different way.

A loving God can not pour out death and destruction on the objects of his love. The image of God as the cosmic dictator gleefully watching and waiting for an opportunity to pour out his vengeance on any person or nation that dares to defy his sovereign authority is a grossly inadequate concept of God. God is concerned with each of his children and wants for them only what is best. His basic nature is love and he is powerless to act in any other way.

Secondly, God's power is limited by the nature of the universe that he created. The universe is orderly and functions according to predictable, discernible laws. As far as we look into the vast reaches of space there is order and consistency. As deeply as we probe into the minute realm of the atom, there too is regularity and harmony. The wise creator of an infinite universe so saturated with order and reliability would hardly interrupt its harmony on the desire or even the need of a man or a nation. God will reveal to many the mysteries of nature and will teach us to enter into harmony with nature, but he will not interrupt or interfere with its laws upon our request. He made it orderly and he respects the order which he established.

Third, God is limited by the nature of dynamic creativity. The static ordering of the physical universe would be an awesome feat. But the adventure of dynamic creativity which involves life and living things engaged in the on-going process of evolution is far more spectacular. Our best science reveals an ever-expanding universe. Dynamic creativity is everywhere.

Dynamic creativity is flexible. It is becoming. This indicates a willingness on God's part to learn by experience – by trial and error if you would. Living things possess an element of freedom, a degree of choice called spontaneity. This spontaneity increases as the level of complexity increases. This means that the reaction of any living thing to life situations cannot be predicted with absolute accuracy even by God. Some species make the necessary changes and adaptations to stay in tune with their environment and survive. Other species adapt too slowly, refuse to adapt at all or adapt incorrectly. They are out of tune with the life force of the universe and fail in the struggle for survival. This orderly process of evolution through natural selection and the survival of the fittest is an expression of God's dynamic creativity. It is God's adventure in becoming. He does not arbitrarily interfere with it.

Most acutely, God's power is limited by human freedom. The human being represents the highest point in evolutionary development that we know about. At the highest level of complexity, human beings enjoy the greatest degree of spontaneity. This range of response and exercise in freedom are so noticeably unique as to set humans apart from all other animals in a class of their own. God makes us free rational creatures capable of relating to him positively in co-operation and also capable of relating to him negatively in rebellion and conflict. God could have made us the tools of his fancy and necessarily obedient to his will, but then we would have been incapable of love or creativity or entering into meaningful relationships. God wanted to make us like Him, capable of loving. In his creation God committed himself to the principle of human freedom. God is creative love and wants us to share the joy of loving and the privilege of creativity. Because of his commitment to freedom, God will not force his will on any person. He will not interfere with human's freedom even when it is as grossly misused as it was by Hitler in his massacre of the Jews or by the evil men who convicted and crucified Jesus Christ. Man's abuse of his freedom is the major source of most of the evil, conflict and suffering in our world. God doesn't want these things to happen, but because of his devotion to human freedom, he is powerless to stop them.

Is God all powerful? NO! He is limited by his nature – by the order and consistency of the universe he established, most severely, by his generous gift of freedom to mankind.

Man's destiny is not determined by the will of God. Fate and the will of God are not synonymous. The fickle finger of fate moves in action quite independently and often contrary to the will of God for his children. The vicissitudes of chance, so often blamed on God, are really the result of an intricate interplay between the laws of the universe and human freedom. God's will for every one of his children is a wholesome, happy, abundant life. He does not will crippling disease, fatal accidents, the horrors of war, or natural disaster. These things happen because of the natural orderly functioning of the universe or because of the misuse of human freedom or because of conflict between human freedom and the natural order.

God cannot be blamed for war, with all of its heartache, suffering, and loss. War is the clear result of the misappropriation of human freedom. Men or nations choose to dominate others to satisfy their lust for power or land. They choose to resolve their difference in violence. But none of this is the will of God. He wants all men to live together peacefully as brothers, but he cannot force his will upon them. It is not God's fault when an only son, the one his parents had lived for and dreamed about and loved all those years, loses his life in some distant battlefield. God is not to blame when a promising young athlete loses a leg in combat. Nor is he responsible when innocent children are injured or killed in a combat zone. All this is not failure on God's part! It is failure on man's part - men refusing to use their freedom responsibly. Yet, again and again the bereaved, out of the depths of their agony, cry out, "Why did God do this to me? Why my son? Why my husband?"

Nor should crippling or incurable disease be attributed to God. It is not God's will that people suffer. Disease is a part of the natural order. It fits usefully into the greater scheme of things. It is a part of natural selection and the survival of the fittest. When disease attacks persons it is our task to control and eliminate it.

God has given us the potential to do this. As the Psalmist expresses it, "thou madest him to have dominion over the worlds of thy hands; thou hast put all things under his feet." We can control and eliminate disease. This is what God wants us to do. Medical science has made amazing strides in recent years but even greater strides could have been made if we had tried harder. Our values have been confused. Business executives, entertainment figures, and professional athletes are paid enormous salaries while college or university professors and medical researchers barely eek out an existence. We spend far more for weapons' development than we do on cancer research. When a mother looks into the casket at the body of her sweet little child who died of leukemia, it is not God whom she should castigate. It is man – his confused values, the misdirection of his abilities - his failure to fully realize the potentials within him.

God should not be berated for accidents that happen. Accidents happen when people forget or defy the laws of nature. To say, "Why did God let it happen?" is a futile query. God didn't want it to happen but he was powerless to keep it from happening. We put our trust in machines that were built for profit more than for safety; that are serviced by men who work more for wages than for the joy of constructive service and are operated by people whose minds are cluttered by multitudinous conflicts, pressures, and tensions. It's a wonder that so many survive in this complex technological jungle as do. Accidents happen because people are oblivious to the forces of nature. They overestimate the technological excellence of their equipment. They trust to their luck and take un-warranted chances with their lives and the lives of others. Most accidents reflect a misuse of human freedom and its inevitable conflict with the natural order. God can not interfere. He can only suffer with us. If we will listen to Him, God will try to protect us by encouraging us to respect natural law, to recognize human frailty, and to let all our actions be motivated by love and concern for others in the human family. But how few there are who listen!

Even what Theologians call natural evil is not willed by God. Floods, storms, and earthquakes that wreak havoc with man and his creations – these are not the malevolent designs of an angry or jealous God. These natural occurrences would happen if no men were there to observe them. But, then they would not be natural evil or disaster. It is the unfortunate coincidence of man's location in an area of natural violence that creates disasters. This is hardly God's fault. God feels our suffering with us but cannot intervene in our behalf.

God is not the master planner who, in eternity prior to creation, completely programmed the lives of every human being designating some for happiness, some for sorrows - scheduling some for glory, some for shame. Such a self-centered manipulative Deity is hardly worthy of our respect and devotion. He would warrant only on contempt and our pity for we the creatures would be more righteous, more imaginative, and more creative than the one who made us. The glory of God is seen in his creation of man in his own image, sharing his creativity, his imagination, and his freedom. God is not the dictator of human destiny, but the experimenter with human freedom.

Human freedom is what makes it possible for us to rise above the animal level. It makes us capable of relationship with another and with God. It makes life interesting and challenging. The element of freedom and the potential or relationship make eternal life something to be desired.

It is true that in gambling with human freedom, God had to sacrifice, not only his omnipotence (total power), but a degree of his omniscience (total knowledge) as well. He obviously believed that the experiment was worthy of the sacrifice. If man is truly free, God cannot know for certain what choices he is going to make. God's knowledge of the future is at best a good guess. In the misuse of his freedom, man often makes choices which God did not plan or want. The purpose of God for his creation has been delayed and frustrated again and again by man's rebellion. Yet God maintains his commitment to freedom because that is love's way.

It should be clear then that God is not the cosmic controller of man's fate and destiny. God is not independent of time. There are those who try to re-enforce their belief in God's omniscience by declaring that God is independent of time. He lives in the realm of eternity and from that vantage point can see all of time from its beginning to its ending, simultaneously. The past, the present, and the future, as we know them, are all present to God. If this is true, then God deserves our sympathy rather than our worship for his existence is utterly devoid of meaning, excitement, or fulfillment.

To assume that God is independent of time is to misunderstand the definition of time and eternity. Time is the measure of eternity. It is the moment by moment succession of events. Eternity is the infinite continuation of time in both directions. God has experienced eternity past but the future is as much future for him as it is for us.

If we should develop a meaningful concept of who God is, it is imperative that we keep His limitations in mind as well. Much of the hostility or ambivalence that people feel toward religion arise from their unrealistic expectations of God. When we know what God cannot do, we can accept him as He is. We can love him for the good world that he has made and for our share in it. We can begin to cultivate our own potential to love. In so doing we perceive and participate in the ground of our being – the creative force of love from which we spring.

Chapter IV
A Working Hypothesis / A Rational Christian Paradigm

> *"Believe nothing on the faith of traditions, even though they have been held in honor for many generations, and in diverse places. Do not believe a thing because many speak of it. Do not believe on the faith of the sages of the past… Believe nothing on the sole authority of your masters or priests. After examination believe what you yourself have tested and found to be reasonable, and confirm your conduct thereto."*
>
> Gautama Buddah

AN EARLY AND PERSISTENT QUESTION FOR HUMAN BEINGS is how can I discover and know the truth? An even deeper question is how can I know anything for sure? In the sixth century BCE, Pythagoras believed that mathematical truths were absolute. He is most famous for the Pathagorium Theorem about right triangles that the square of the two smaller sides will always be equal to the square of the longest segment. He did not make that discovery through experiment, trial and error. It came to him intuitively. Building on the absolute truth of mathematical functions, Pythagoras believed that the absolute power at the heart of the universe was The Ultimate Mathematician, and that the whole of the universe was a function of mathematical relationships. This was his hypothesis about God and it defined his spirituality and modified his behavior.

Late in the Sixth Century B.C.E., Socrates became a prominent philosopher in Athens. Socrates never wrote any books but he inspired others to write down his ideas. His most famous student was Plato who wrote numerous treatises. Many of his writings were dialogues between Socrates and other persons. Socrates' theme was that the unexamined life is not worth living. He claimed to know nothing for certain - no absolute truth. He believed that by introspection and dialogue with other searchers for truth that more truth could be discovered. Whatever truth we know is a feeble resemblance of ultimate truth that exists on a higher plane.

Religion claims to have absolute truths because it is revealed to the founder or leader directly by a higher power. Ultimate truth was revealed to Moses and so recorded in the Torah (first five books of Hebrew Scripture) Ultimate truth was revealed to the Buddha, Zoroaster, Mohammed, or other great religious leaders. For most Christians, ultimate truth is revealed through Jesus as recorded in the Bible.

The problem with these ultimate truths is that they cannot be ultimate because they disagree, and each of the revelations is affirmed as the only true message. All others are at least wrong, and at worse, evil.

We have seen that human beings seem to have an innate propensity to be religious. Religions tend to be absolutist, that is their religion is right and all other religions are wrong. Even within religious communities like Christianity, one group or faction will insist that their understanding of the Faith is the only true or proper understanding, while all the many other groups are wrong!

Many religious people are willing to engage in war, terrorist action, torture and intimidation to prove their religion or their faction of a religion is an ultimate truth. Revealed religion can be dangerous and destructive.

As Socrates affirmed that the unexamined life is not worth living, I would assert to take any religion unexamined by reason and history is not worth following. The absolutist claims of any religion should be examined for positive effectiveness and social utility. A rational person who responds to the intuitive urge toward spirituality should develop their own working hypothesis about God and life. A working hypothesis is not absolute or exclusive. It is subject to revision based on reason, experience and history. It is a way of thinking about God, life and people - it is a religious frame of reference.

My working hypothesis is about origins, relationships and purpose… about my God concept…my religious paradigm. It is primarily rooted in the life and teachings of Jesus described in the Gospels of the New Testament and the positive elements of the Hebrew Scriptures that inspired Jesus. This approach to Christianity is relational, rational and respectful. It does not claim to be absolute Truth but provides a functional philosophy for the physical, spiritual and social challenges of life. This working hypothesis becomes a practical guide for life decisions, life style, and goals. The values that guide this approach to life are love, rational consistency, creativity and productivity.

Within this frame of reference, God is that personal dynamic, creative Spirit responsible for the emergence of our universe and all who inhabit it. That Power at the heart of the universe is Love. This Love permeates all of creation and moves it towards progress and fulfillment.

This working hypothesis about God is rooted in a number of informational sources. A major source of information for human beings on all subjects is our physical senses: our sight, hearing, touch, taste and smell. When we are born, much of our brain is a blank slate, an empty book, in which we write the history of our sensory experiences. Our early experiences inform us about the world around us. We learn to distinguish ourselves from the world around us, and soon we learn to manipulate that world to meet our needs. We recognize that we are not alone. There are other people around us. We need their help to survive and hopefully they will respond to our needs. We learn to communicate with people through the miracle of language. When we learn to read, we are able to tap into the collective memory of the people who have lived before us. There was probably a time in our species history long, long ago when our senses of smell, taste and touch were as important to our survival as those of sight and hearing. Today, where the most dominate senses are seeing and hearing, our sensory experiences are steadily compiling information in our memory which helps us make informed decisions.

How can our senses tell us anything about God? Human people from earliest time presumed that there was some spiritual force responsible for and in control of the physical universe. This is not a sensory experience, but an intuitive conclusion. If we share in that intuitive conclusion that there is a creative force originating and sustaining the universe, then all that our senses tell us about the world around us is inferential information about the Creator.

First, we will consider the known facts on which this hypothesis is based. As mentioned before, our five senses, sight, hearing, touch, taste, and smell are the primary sources of all of the knowledge which we possess. Throughout our lives these senses provide us with most of the vital information necessary for survival, growth and fulfillment. The major portion of all we know comes to us through our senses.

What do our senses tell us about God? If God is spirit, there is nothing our senses can tell us directly about Him. But if we assume that He is in the creative force originating and sustaining the universe, all that our senses tell us of the world around us is information about Him. As Saint Paul put it, "what men can know about God is plain to them. God himself made it plain to them. Ever since God created the world, his invisible qualities, both his eternal power and his divine nature, have been clearly seen. Men can perceive them in the things that God has made." (Romans 1:19-20 NKJV) Centuries earlier the Psalmist expressed it this way, 'The heavens declare the glory of God; and the firmament showeth his handiwork.' (Psalm 19:1 KJV) "O Lord, our Lord your greatness is seen in all the world!...When I look at the sky, which you have made, at the moon and stars which you set in their places – what is man that you think of him; mere man, that you care for him? Yet you made him inferior only to yourself, you crowned him with glory and honor. You appointed him ruler over everything you made…O Lord, our Lord, your greatness is seen in all the world." (Ps 8, TEV)

The beauty of nature bespeaks a God who appreciates beauty. The vastness of space indicates a God great beyond our ability to fully comprehend. The intricate balance in all of nature reveals superb craftsmanship. The process of evolution is an indicator of infinite foresight. The storm and the earthquake appall us with awesome power. The order and consistency of natural law point to a consistent, reliable creator. The miracle of life and reproduction assures us of the living presence of a creative dynamic force in the world.

In another way, our senses tell us about God. Through our senses we learn what other people have believed about God. With our eyes we see the images they have worshipped, the temples they have erected, and the rituals which they perform. What we do not see directly, we can read about in books of Theology, History, and Anthropology. Reading makes available to us an avalanche of books and documents declaring and defending people's faith in the gods or in God. With our ears we hear the testimony of people around us about God. With our eyes we see lives dramatically changed because of a new religious experience. We hear the sound of praise adoration offered to God in Worship. We smell the fragrance of incense and eat the sacramental food.

We may never see, hear, smell, taste or touch God, but these senses do make inference about God as experienced in nature, and about ideas and practices of various people in response to their ideas about God.

The second source of information about God is the mind. The human mind is a wonderful and mysterious instrument. Because of our ability to remember and to communicate to another, we are able to pass to successive generations the experiences and conclusions of the past. Our ability to reason enables us to take the information provided by our senses, evaluate it, integrate it, and deduce from it further truth. To what our ancestors believed about God, we add our experiences and conclusions and should arrive at an increasing functional understanding.

It is, therefore, preposterous to claim that our ancestors knew more of God than do we. Any Christian Church tied to the idea that ultimate truth was expressed in the creeds of the first to fourth centuries, blindly disregards the fact that greater truth is progressively revealed to the diligent seeker. Organized religions almost always claim to possess absolute truth. Humans are not capable of absolute truth. All truth for us is partial truth. In Paul's first letter to the church at Corinth in the N.T. (Ch 13), he says, in his famous description of love, that our knowledge is only partial, but when we are elevated to a higher place, we shall see clearly. It is unfortunate that later Christian leaders assumed that their ideas were absolute truth and anyone who saw things differently was evil.

A God who can be fully understood and perfectly described by the theologians of the early centuries is an infinitesimally small God. If all the people who have invested years and even lifetimes in meditation and study about God during the past fifteen centuries can do no more than defend and affirm the beliefs of the past, then Theology is the most decadent of all studies and their God is a subject totally unworthy of so much attention.

The human mind has the potential for discovering new truth and is possessed with an insatiable thirst for new knowledge. This is evidenced by the colossal developments in the fields of science, technology, and medicine. If the powers of the mind are freed from the shackles of the past, they can discover equally amazing truth about the ultimate force of the universe. The mind, honestly and diligently used, is an important source of information about God.

It is not easy to free our minds from the shackles of the past. Many of them are infused into the very structure of Christianity. To challenge its authenticity and to liberate oneself from its grip, is to invite criticism. One must be prepared to be labeled a heretic, a radical, or even an atheist. Rejection, even persecution, is the reward organized religion reserves for those who rock the boat or shake the foundations. The death of Socrates and the crucifixion of Jesus are classic examples of the price exacted from those who shatter the fetters of ignorance and lead people in the path of truth.

Fear has long been a shackle that constricts the minds of men. The witch doctor ruled the primitive tribe by fear. The sacred must not be questioned. The "Holy Other" must not be probed or investigated. Those who endeavor to scale the walls of heaven shall certainly be scattered and destroyed. This is the implication of the story of the Tower of Babel in the Book of Genesis. People were going to build a tower that would reach to heaven. In anger and fear over such human ambition, God confused people's language and scattered them all over the face of the earth. (Genesis 11:1-9) Many other stories in the Bible are designed to make one cringe in fear before a holy unapproachable and unpredictable God. One of the most notable of these is the story of Uzzah. (2 Sam 6:3-11). The Ark of God was being transported by oxcart to Jerusalem. The cart hit a bump in the road and it appeared that the ark was about to fall into the mud. Uzzah reached out his hand to steady it, "And the anger of the Lord was kindled against Uzzah, and God smote him there for his error, and there he died by the Ark of God." (1 Chronicles 13:9 SV) Even the New Testament describes fear tactics in the management of the earthly church. (Acts 5:1-11) The early Christian formed a commune. People sold their possessions and put in a common treasury. The story was widely circulated that a couple, Anamas and Sapphira, lied to Peter about the price of their property which they had sold. They wanted to keep a little for themselves. They must not have been completely sold in this community property bit. For their lie, they fell dead before Peter. "And great fear came upon all the Church, and upon as many as heard these things." (Acts 5:11 RSV) In true loyalty to Peter's example, the church has continued to threaten people with untimely death, and the fires of Hell if they didn't obey the rules and accept as absolute the teachings of the church. The very last chapter of the last book of the Bible says that if anybody adds anything to this book, God will add to him the plagues described in the book and if anybody takes anything out of this book, God will erase his name from the book of Life (Revelations 22:18,19). Organized Religions love to use fear to control people.

Another fetter that limits the utilization of our mental capacities is the fable of inferiority. God is infinite and we are finite. "For my thoughts are not your thoughts, neither are your ways my ways, saith the Lord. For as the heavens are higher than the earth, so are my ways higher than your ways, and my thoughts than your thoughts." (Isaiah 55:8, RSV) He is totally transcendent - so far beyond our ability to understand that we should not even try. We should blindly accept what we have been told by the Church without question and without doubt. Everything that is obviously contradictory must be accepted as paradoxical truth. All other doctrines that don't make sense are to be cherished as "holy mysteries."

Another encumbrance to free thinking is the church's obsession with apologetics. It is assumed that a set of doctrines and creeds to be true. Then we exert all of our mental energies defending these sacred beliefs. This obsession in Christianity had its origin as early as the beginning of the second century (C.E). The first century church emphasized the task of bringing people into a new dynamic relationship with the living God. Right relationship was their concern. But by the time that the letters to Timothy and Titus were written, the emphasis had shifted from right relationship to right belief and correct doctrine. A faith that leads people into a right relationship with the living God does not need apologetics. It produces living proof of its validity.

Freed from these restrictions, our minds can begin to probe the depths for sound information about God. In this quest, a few practical guidelines are useful. The first is simplicity. There is nothing good or sacred about complexity. Avoid complex doctrines as you would a plague. We should keep our working hypothesis about God as simple as possible.

Another important guideline in our thoughts about God is

inclusiveness. We do not have all the answers. Christians do not have a corner on truth. We should consider the wisdom of all religions. The discoveries of all intellectual disciplines, psychology, medicine, philosophy and anthropology to mention only a few, should be given consideration.

Our thoughts should be bound together by strong cords of consistency. We should make a conscious effort to eliminate all internal inconsistencies in our thought. For example, if we believe that God is love, we should not also believe that God is jealous or would be vindictive or destructive toward his enemies. A God of love could not commit genocide or order his followers to do so!

Most of all, our working hypothesis should work for us. Believing in a positive God of Love should inspire us to be positive, creative and compassionate persons. Our God concept should lead us to a better and happier life and should inspire us to help others find the same.

The third source of information about God is religious experience. This may be an intuitive awareness of a higher power, a feeling of being transported to a spiritual plane. It is described as a personal experience of the living God. This experience may come to us in a dream or vision. It may occur during a worship experience or in a special natural setting. The Prophet Isaiah describes his experiences of God in Isaiah 6:1-8. Job's experience of God is described in Chapters 38-42 of the Book of Job. Every person experiences God in his own way. It is true that this information is totally subjective. It cannot be objectively scrutinized and tested. It often cannot even be objectively put into words. This is spirit to Spirit contact; the human spirit in direct contact with the Ultimate Source of our being. The validity of such experiences can only be supported by the impact they have had on the life of the person having this experience. Saint Paul was completely changed after his confrontation with Jesus on the road to Damascus. Saint Francis of Assisi was never the same after he heard God speak to him. John Wesley was dynamically different after his "heart warming" experience. Hopeless alcoholics have been transformed into happy useful citizens by a personal experience of The Devine. Thousands of people who were sick of body and of soul have been miraculously healed when they came into personal contact with the living God.

Religious experience of this nature cannot help being a learning experience. God reveals directly, person to person, spirit to spirit, the truth about himself. This mistaken opinion that direct revelation came only to the writers of Holy Scripture or that it was limited to the dispensation of these writers, cannot be defended logically. God progressively reveals more and more of himself to people as they are increasingly able and willing to accept the revelation. We do not know all there is to know about God and if future generations profit by our experience, it is certain that they will know more about God than we.

Using our senses, our minds, and the progressive intuition which God provides, we arrive at a personal understanding of the nature and limitations of God. Following this method, I have developed the working hypothesis stated at the beginning of this chapter. God is that personal, dynamic, creative spirit responsible for the emergence of our universe and all who inhabit it. The essence, the nature, the very being of God is universal ultimate LOVE. This love permeates all of creation and moves it toward progress and fulfillment. This is my religious frame of reference – my sacred paradigm.

The remaining chapters will develop this fundamental hypothesis in greater detail.

Chapter V

God Is a Gambler

"It is surely the most breathtaking affirmation in scripture! God is Love!...it is by far the most exciting statement about God to be found in either the Bible or any other literature in the world."

Geddes MacGregor (He Who Lets Us Be)

LOVE IS CREATIVE AND DYNAMIC BUT NEITHER OF THESE exists apart from risk. Love always involves gambling. When a young couple stands before the altar of the church to be joined in holy matrimony they accept each other for better or for worse, for richer or poor, in sickness or in health, till death severs the relationship. What a gamble! They have only known each other for a year, occasionally several years and sometimes for only a month. I talked to a young couple just recently who had known each other for only one month and they were fully prepared to take this risk. This is the gamble of love. It is amazing how often people come out winners. The tragic number of losers at the game of love is growing at an appalling rate. One marriage in two ends in divorce. It is highly doubtful that one out of the two remaining is a truly happy marriage, but people still marry and they will continue to take the risk because that is love's way.

Since God at the very essence of his being is love, he, too, is involved in the risk of dynamic creativity. When he made human beings in his own image, he took the colossal gamble. He had no way of knowing how it would turn out and once it was done, he was powerless to interfere. He had made them intelligent beings and endowed him with the right of free choice. He could only hope that in response to his love, people would make the right choices. He must have known, from the start, that this would not always happen. But human freedom and dignity meant more to God than blind obedience to his will. He loved human beings and wanted them to experience his love and to be capable of loving. Free will is a prerequisite to the potential of loving. Love motivated God to create and dictated the pattern of his creation.

The outcome of God's great gamble varies with each individual. Every person is a potential winner. He has within him the capability of maturing to an adult understanding that love is the essence of life. That in sharing and giving one finds wholeness and fulfillment. But so few of us arrive at such an understanding. We frustrate the intent of God to share with us, life abundant. We get hung up at some early stage of our development and miss so much of the point and purpose of life.

All too often religion has contributed to this arrested development. The inadequate concepts of God and the degrading image of man which many Christians hold, have caused people to be satisfied with their development. Instead of prodding them to improve in the art and joy of loving, it has sedated them with the hope of "pie in the sky by and by," or it has crystallized them in the bigoted opinion that they have already achieved righteousness and the rest of the world can be damned.

At its best, religion is an instrument of the life-force of love that motivates people to grow in relationships - a positive relationship with other people, with God, and with the universe in which we find ourselves. We should not be satisfied with any religion or any God that falls short of this. From the moment that man emerged from the evolutional process, God has been drawing us toward wholeness. The record of our feeble and faltering responses is reflected in the religions of man past and present.

God's gamble with freedom is nowhere more vividly depicted than in the Garden of Eden story. The real impact of this story is grasped most clearly when it is understood symbolically. Adam, in the original language, is the generic word for mankind and Eve for womankind. They symbolize the human race. The Garden of Eden symbolizes God's full sharing of himself and his creation with man. The serpent represents human immaturity and the remnant of our animal nature. The forbidden fruit represents egocentric pride and humanity's overt concern with survival and self-preservation. The decision faced was the decision to give oneself in response to love or to isolate oneself in hostile independence. The choice was Adam and Eve's to make. God wanted them to choose love but, committed to the gamble of freedom as he is, God would not force his will upon them.

Consider the Biblical story more completely. Adam and Eve had been given the garden to use and enjoy. There they enjoyed intimate fellowship with God. Their part in this relationship of love was to avoid the use of the fruit of one tree as God had requested. This request gave them personal involvement in the loving relationship. Eve went to that tree and looked at it. Its fruit looked very enticing. The serpent said, "The fruit is good to eat. Have some." But Eve said, "God instructed us not to eat of this fruit." The serpent replied, "Do you know why? It was because he knew that in the day that you eat of this fruit you will be equal with (and independent of) him". There was the choice - loving relationship or arrogant hostile independence. Eve chose independence and ate the fruit. Then she talked her husband into joining her. When God came to have fellowship with them, they went and hid. They had chosen arrogant independence and were no longer capable of relationship. They could no longer give themselves in love. This egocentric attitude even shattered their relationship with each other. They became keenly aware of their difference sexually. The immaturity of their state is seen in their refusal to accept responsibility for their action. Adam blamed Eve and God. "It was that woman that You gave me. She made me eat!" Eve blamed the serpent and God. "It was that serpent that you made. The serpent made me eat!" God condemned the serpent (their immaturity) and helped them to a partial relationship with each other by giving them clothing of animal skins to hide their differences. Then he made them leave the Garden and put an angel at the entrance to forbid their return. Remember that the Garden was the symbol of God giving himself in love. The story is misleading at this point. God did not put them out of the Garden. They walled themselves out by choosing egocentric isolation and making relationship impossible. The angel that forbade their return was their own isolation and fear that kept them from giving themselves in loving response to God's love. That is one way to make some rational sense of this story.

This beautiful story is not the accurate account of an historical event. It is instead the existential description of man's eternal predicament. God offers himself continually to every person in love but he does not force himself upon us. The choice is ours and we are free to decide for ourselves. We can respond to God's love by giving ourselves in loving relationship or we can react to his love in egocentric independence. If we are afraid to give ourselves in love, we build walls of isolation around us that separate us from the Ground of Our Being and from one another. We are lost in our self-made hell of lonely isolation. Salvation only comes to us when in an act of faith we tear down the walls of separation and let love come-when we dare to share ourselves with God and our fellow human beings in warm loving relationships.

Salvation then is constantly available to all men and has been since the beginning. From the beginning, God has been giving himself in love, wanting - even longing for man's acceptance of that love. He has been hoping that the anxiety, the pain, the tragedy of man's out-of-tuneness will motivate him to seek a better life. He has enveloped every person with his love so that when a person opens the wall just a crack, God floods him with love and light.

But why do people shut themselves off from love and the infinite possibilities of life? Why did Adam and Eve make the choice of arrogant independence instead of a loving relationship? Why is the symbolic story relived again and again in your life and in mine? It is not God's will! It is not the inevitable choice of a destructively oriented creature. It is not the only choice open to a depraved and fallen race. It is a choice we make freely. It is the wrong choice and God does everything within his power to show us that when we realize our error, we are perfectly free and fully capable of correcting it. To the extent that we learn to choose love and life, God wins and we win in his gamble with freedom.

The reason why we make so many wrong choices is quite simple. It is because we have not matured as human beings. We live too much out of our animal instincts and our sub-human concerns. The basic instinct of the animal kingdom is survival. The fundamental law in that realm is the survival of the fittest. Egocentric concern is the key to continued existence. But this is not true for rational creatures. In the world of free intelligent spiritual beings, the laws of life and growth and meaningful existence are much different. The secret of life for human beings is love. Life's fulfillment comes to us through warm meaningful relationships with others and with God. Confucius advised us not do to others what we do not want done to us. Jesus suggested that we give ourselves in love to one another. Even give yourself in love to your enemies. He who would save his life (egocentric independence) shall loose it. .But he who gives his life in loving relationships shall find it. John S. Mill in the mid 19th Century put it this way, "It is every individual's obligation as well as his pleasure to promote the well being of his fellows."

This is the lesson that Adam and Eve had not learned yet. They were afraid to give themselves in a loving relationship. They lacked the courage to be mature human beings. Out of their animalistic instinct for survival, they chose hostile equality. They could not accept God's loving gift of himself because it involved a degree of giving on their part. The lesson of love, fundamental as it is, is not easily learned.

The error in Adam and Eve's choice is demonstrated in the next Biblical story - that of Cain and Abel. The details of the story are somewhat foggy. It seems that God accepted the worship of Abel more than that of Cain.

Knowing that God accepts and loves all men equally, we understand that this opinion was part of Cain's imagination. He refused to give himself in love to his brother. He was, therefore, blind to God's love and acceptance of him. He looked on his brother as a competitor - a threat to his happiness and fulfillment. Acting out of selfishness and jealousy and abiding by the animal law of survival of the fittest, he killed his brother; only to find that instead of improving his relationship with God and giving him greater happiness, his choice of arrogant independence has broadened the gap between him and God and between him and his fellowmen. He felt rejected by God and afraid of his associates.

Cain's attitude is clearly expressed in the interchange between he and God after the murder of Able. God asked, “Where is your brother Able?” Cain answered, “How should I know? Am I my brother's keeper?” Graphic expression of egocentric isolation - Cain cared only about Cain. This is an excusable attitude for animals but not for human beings. For people, who should have outgrown the childish idea that they are the center of the universe, this is a self-destructive attitude. Somewhere between the ages of four and eight, the normal human being becomes fully aware of the existence of other human beings like him. These people have feelings and needs like his and he can relate to them positively or negatively. If he chooses to disregard these obvious facts and bulldozes his way through life as if he were the only person that matters, he brings tragedy, suffering and pain to the people around him and ultimately destruction to himself. Cain is the symbol of this unproductive approach to life.

Both of these stories illustrate our reluctance to give ourselves in loving relationships to God or to other persons. The extent to which we overcome that reluctance, is at once the measure of our maturity and the key to our happiness and fulfillment. When one dares to give himself in love, life becomes an exciting adventure in transformation. Our life is transformed from a dull, empty existence to a thrilling encounter with God. Miraculous changes occur in our lives and in the lives of those we love. We enjoy a new in-tuneness with the life force of the universe as we participate in the abundant life God intends for every person.

God has been revealing this truth from the beginning but we have been so slow to learn. Socrates had glimpses of it in his challenge to the youth of Athens. In Plato's Crito, Socrates says, "We ought not to retaliate or render evil for evil to anyone, whatever evil we may have suffered from him." Confucius saw the need to respect the feelings and needs of others. He said that a man without charity in his heart had no religion; that he is out of harmony with life. Ancient Hindu scriptures teach that "true religion is to love, as God has loved them, all things whether great or small. Those who worship me with love, I love; they are in me, and I in them." The ninth perfection in Buddhism is loving-kindness. "As water quenches the thirst of the good and bad alike, and cleanses them of dust and impurity, so also shall you treat your friend and foe alike with loving kindness."

The prophets and seers of the ancient Hebrews often proclaimed God's message of love. One of the most widely known of these instructions is, "Thou shall love thy neighbor as thyself." Similar to this is the injunction in Deuteronomy 15:11 to open wide your hand to your brother, to the needy and to the poor. The Proverbs suggest, "Better is a dinner of herbs where love is, than a stalled ox and hatred therewith." Jeremiah understood God's love when he said, "The Lord hath appeared. . . unto me, saying, 'Yea, I have loved thee with an everlasting love; therefore with loving-kindness have I drawn thee.'" The prophet Hosea in a beautiful parable of his own relationship with his wife, Gomer, demonstrated the nature of God's love. Even though Gomer deserted him again and again for adulterous relationships, he continued to love and forgive her until love saved her. This is the way that God loves every person who ever lives. From the beginning, He has been endeavoring to communicate this love to those who would listen.

These great men of ancient times caught a glimpse of God's love. They began to understand the basic issues of life. They represent high points in man's struggle toward wholeness and maturity. They reflect some of the dividends in God's investment of love. They kept alive the hope that all was not lost in God's colossal gamble. And, indeed, it wasn't. For one day in the hill country of Palestine, God got a winner!

Chapter VI
God Gets a Winner

"Jesus is what God means by 'Man',
He is what man means by 'God'."
J.S. Whale, Christian Doctrine

"Love is patient and kind; love is not jealous . . . or selfish, or irritable; love does not keep a record of wrongs; . . . love never gives up; its faith, hope and patience never fail."
I Corinthians 13:4-7 (TEV)

HOW ENCOURAGING IT IS TO KNOW THAT THIS BEAUTIFUL description of love by Saint Paul is also a description of God. In risking the colossal gamble of giving human beings freedom, God demonstrates unconditional love. God has been most patient and kind with humankind. God had enduring faith and his hope that people would eventually respond fully to his love. He has never given up. He has kept calling to every human being trying to lead them to the abundant life, to the full happy meaningful life available in loving relationships. As we have noted many of the prophets, sages, and pious people of the ancient world were open to the spiritual realm and diligently sought to know and share meaningful truth. There were striking similarities in the truth they discovered, but ideas about God and the supreme importance of love were mixed and inconsistent. As the centuries rolled on, it seemed doubtful that anybody would fully respond to God's call. But, since love never gives up, God kept on trying.

Finally in the hills of Palestine in the days of Caesar Augustus, God's gamble paid off. God got a real winner!

A young man named Jesus (a common name in those days) was born to a pious young Jewish couple. His father, Joseph, was a carpenter by trade. Both Mary, his mother, and Joseph were deeply religious people. They had not received classical theological training. But they knew a God who guided them by dreams, or visions, and spoke to them through Scripture and their religious traditions. They loved God with all their hearts. They loved each other deeply. They loved life and worked at loving their neighbor as they loved themselves. Naturally, the child born of their love grew up in an atmosphere of love and devotion.

He felt loved and accepted by his parents. Through their love, their faith, and example, he came to feel God's love and total acceptance. It was in the security of such an atmosphere that he experienced his freedom as a human individual. As all "Adams" before him, he faced the choice between self-centered isolation with its rejection of love or the sharing of oneself in response to love. Confident in the love he had experienced, he chose to give himself in loving response. He shared himself with his parents and with God and experienced the joy of loving relationships. The rewards of loving reinforced the proper use of his freedom until giving himself in love became the habit pattern of his life.

Jesus' sensitivity to people and his understanding of God were amazing to the religious leaders in Jerusalem when he visited the temple with his parents at the age of twelve. His childhood and youth are summarized beautifully in Luke's Gospel; and "Jesus increased in wisdom and stature, and in favor with God and man." Luke 2:12 (RSV) We have no detailed information about this period in Jesus' life. We do not know how much formal education he received. We know that he knew well the ancient scriptures of the Hebrews because he often quoted and interpreted them during his later ministry. Jesus was probably an outstanding student at the Sabbath Synagogue School. It is likely that he was strongly influenced by the Essenes (a disciplined order of religious enthusiasts) or similar groups. The writer of Luke suggests that Jesus and John the Baptist were cousins. Scholars have long thought that John the Baptist represented the Essene religious tradition. Jesus and John may have spent some time in isolated religious fellowships like the Qumran Community cultivating the disciplines of meditation and prayer.

At about the age of thirty, under the influence of John the Baptist, Jesus decided to launch into a public ministry. He chose the religious symbol of baptism to declare to all, his intention to embark on a new spiritual adventure.

As he was coming up out of the water he had a traumatic religious experience. He felt a special empowering unity with God and a deep sense of God's approval of him and God's call to proclaim the good news of God's Love. It was his task to initiate the reign of God and demonstrate how wonderful it is to be partners with God. He accepted the call and committed himself to an intimate partnership with God to speak for God to all who would listen. After his baptism he spent several weeks in the wilderness in preparatory meditation and prayer. Here in communion with God, he worked out the strategy of his ministry. The appeal to use the spectacular events to quickly win popularity was strong but he rejected it. The lure of personal gain and the attainment of self-centered goals were very real but his commitment to the way of love was stronger. The temptation to use evil means to achieve positive results presented itself but was rejected. He organized and consolidated his knowledge of truth and opened himself to new revelations from God. He was affirmed and strengthened by angels of God who ministered to him according to Matthew and Mark, the first two Gospels in the New Testament.

Vibrant with excitement over the opportunity to share with many people the good news of God's love, he headed for the cities and towns of Galilee. The theme of Jesus' message was "The time is fulfilled, and the kingdom of God is at hand." Mark 1:15 (RSV) In the synagogue, in his home town of Nazareth he explained his ministry by reading from the prophet Isaiah, "The Spirit of the Lord is upon me, because he has anointed me to preach the gospel to the poor, he hath sent me to heal the brokenhearted, to preach deliverance to the captives, and the recover of sight to the blind. To set at liberty them that are bruised, to preach the acceptable year of the Lord." Luke 4:18,19 (KJV) He went on to preach the finest sermon they had ever heard. They couldn't believe their ears. They said, "Is not this Joseph's son?" When he challenged their short-sightedness and their refusal to see God at work in their midst, the religious leaders and the people were angered. They would have killed him but Jesus left the city before they could. This violent reaction from the religious leaders of his time intensified throughout his public ministry, culminating in his death upon the cross.

The attitude of the people of Nazareth was parochial; other communities in Galilee knew little if anything of Jesus' background. Jesus was warmly received in Capernaum and in many of the other villages and towns in Galilee. The poor and the disadvantaged heard him gladly. He was followed by great crowds in Judea and Jerusalem. There was something different about this man; something that attracted the lonely, the confused, the sick, and the needy.

His appeal to the crowd lay in the depth and sincerity of his love. In every way he radiated his concern for people. Through him people became conscious of God's love and acceptance. He spoke with authority as no man had ever spoken before. It was an authority born out of continuous intimate fellowship with God. When people were around him they felt the presence of God. They couldn't understand this. Jesus explained that they could live in this intimate fellowship with the Father if only they were willing to give themselves in love. But they were afraid to try and the few who did make some effort, did so feebly that no one really understood him. They wanted to be like him but they lacked the courage to love as he did. Therefore they tried to excuse themselves by saying that he was somehow basically different from them.

The aura of the presence of God that always seemed to be with Jesus caused many people to develop and believe a host of superstitious myths about his birth and his childhood. Since they refused to give themselves in love and isolated themselves from God's intimate fellowship, they came to believe that Jesus must have some special tie to God not available to others. Using an explanation common to the ancient world, they developed the beautiful story of the virgin birth with all the wonders of a special star and all the heavenly host singing praise to the half-God, half-human babe. Tradition records other stories about the boy Jesus, and tells how clay birds that he molded flew away. Another tells of a playmate who angered him and when Jesus looked at him the boy fell dead. These later two stories are as grossly inconsistent with the nature of Jesus as the birth stories are inconsistent with the nature of God.

Around all great men a whole body of mythology evolves. Much of it has a stimulus in reality but the stories themselves are not factual. The reality stimulus for the birth stories about Jesus was the intensity and extent of his love and his intimate fellowship with God. These had to be explained supernaturally or people would be obligated to accept him and to try to be like him.

Such stories arose after his death and were either not known or not accepted by many early church leaders. Paul never mentions the virgin birth as a significant doctrine in any of his letters. The earliest Gospel, that of Mark, which was written to encourage and instruct the Christians in Rome, makes no mention of the birth of Jesus. According to many scholars, Peter was one of Mark's primary sources for the Gospel. If the birth stories had been accepted as true by Jesus or by the Apostles, it seems obvious that Peter would have shared them with his Christian friends in Rome. The early Christians accepted Jesus as Lord (leader) and actually patterned their lives after his. They were noted from the way they loved one another. They loved the needy and the slave. They even loved their enemies. They did not need supernatural birth stories to love Jesus and serve him, even die for him. Another reaction to that "sense of the Presence" that people felt when they were with Jesus, was their tendency to worship him. He never accepted such worship. He would lift them to their feet and do whatever he could for them. But whatever was accomplished he would always tell the recipient and those observing that it was God who met their need and that he was only the channel through which God worked. He insisted that he was not different from any other man - that God would work through anybody who was willing to give themselves in love to God and loving concern for their fellowmen. He refused even to be addressed in language usually reserved for God. Two of the Gospels record the story of a young man who came running to Jesus with an urgent spiritual question, "Good Master, what should I do that I may inherit eternal life?" Luke 18:18 (KJV) Before answering this vital question, Jesus felt compelled to clarify another matter. He said to the young man, "Why callest thou me good? There is none good but one, that is God." Luke 18:19 (KJV) Jesus made it very clear that he was not God and was not even to be called "good." Then he answered the young man's question.

The dominating feature in the life and ministry of Jesus was his ability to love. He enjoyed such an intimate fellowship with God that his own human ability to love was magnified and intensified by God's love flowing to him and through him. Jesus loved life. He loved all kinds of people and he enjoyed being with people. He enjoyed parties. His critics called him a wine drinker, a glutton, and a friend of sinners and outcasts. (Matthew 11-19) He became the incarnation of the nature of God. In Jesus' compassion, acceptance and concern for people, mankind got a true glimpse of what God is like. Equally important is the fact that in Jesus' right use of his freedom in loving his fellowmen and God we see man reaching his highest spiritual potential. Since he was human, just as we are, we have within us the potential of being like him. We are called to love as he loved - to be incarnations, the human vessels of Universal Love as he was; to show people everywhere who God really is and what they can be if only they learn how to love.

Love was the theme of the preaching ministry of Jesus. He unified and simplified all the commandments into one command. Thou shall love. The objects of your love should be God, your neighbor and yourself.

A person loves God by accepting his love and responding to it creatively. God loves us continuously whether we are good or bad. When we accept his love and give ourselves in loving relationship to him, all of life takes on new meaning and direction. In intimate fellowship with God we find wisdom, courage, and creative guidance for our lives as Jesus did.

According to Jesus we are to love our neighbors by treating them exactly the way that we would want to be treated. This is putting yourself in the other person's shoes - feeling their pain with them and rejoicing with them when life goes well. It is giving yourself to others, sharing with them, caring about them, accepting them as persons as they are, good or bad, rich or poor. It is giving yourself without demanding anything in return.

Did Jesus really teach us to love ourselves? He said, "If anyone wishes to be a follower of mine, he must leave self behind; he must take up his cross and come over with me. Whoever cares for his own safety is lost; but if a man will let himself be lost for my sake, he will find his true self." Matthew 16:24 (TEV) How can this be interpreted to mean love yourself? We love ourselves by having courage enough to give ourselves in love to others. That is what he meant by losing our lives for his sake. In giving ourselves to others we affirm our own worth as a person. By giving ourselves in loving relationship we find our true self. This free act of loving is the proof that we have risen above the level of animal instincts and survival obsession to the truly human level of relationships between persons and with God.

This message of love was God's message. He tried to communicate this message to every human being but none before Jesus heard it so clearly, declared it so simply, or lived it out so dramatically. In him, God has a winner. Love was not only the theme of his preaching; it was the motivation of his actions as well. His disciples were slow to comprehend and accept his teaching but the impact of his actions were never forgotten.

Outstanding among his characteristics was his warm acceptance of people who found little or no acceptance in the society of their time; the publican, a tax collector, as a reminder of Roman domination, was hated by most of the Jewish populace. To Jesus, they were all human beings in need of love. One of them, the tax collector Matthew, became a disciple. Jesus dined with Zacchaeus, a tax collector, and the transforming power of love changed his life. Jesus was called by his enemies a wine bibber and a friend of publicans and sinners.

His loving acceptance of sinners was demonstrated often. Jesus was teaching in a home when a man sick with palsy was brought to him. The home was so crowded that the bearers of the sick man removed some roof tile and let him down on ropes in front of Jesus. Jesus looked into the man's soul with eyes of compassion and loving acceptance. He perceived instantly the nature of his problem and said, "Your sins are forgiven." Freed from the burden of guilt the man was made whole.

The prostitute, the woman of the street, was an outcast in Jewish society, as she is in every society. Yet even these disgraceful women found love and acceptance from him. Mary Magdalene, identified incorrectly by some 2nd Century Christian writers as a prostitute, found the courage to start a whole new life in the reassuring accepting love of Jesus. Jesus is reputed to have cast out 7 demons from Mary, so she may have had some form of mental illness. Her illness, whatever it was, was healed by the power of love. The Samaritan Woman at the well found strength to turn from a life of sin and waywardness to a more meaningful life when from Jesus she learned that God loved her and cared about her. A woman caught in the act of adultery was dragged before Jesus by her accusers for stoning. Jesus saved her life by asking the blood thirsty group to consider their own lives and then the man who was without sin could cast the first stone. In the presence of Jesus none could claim to be sinless, so one by one they drifted away. Jesus said, "Has no one condemned you?" She said, "No one, sir," and Jesus said unto her, "Neither do I condemn you; go your way, and from now on do not sin again." John 8:10-11 (NRSV) In his acceptance of her as a person, she was inspired to be a better person.

One of the most dramatic examples of Jesus' acceptance of the unacceptable was his experience with the maniac in the land of the Gerasenes. This man was suffering from a severe mental illness which caused him to live among the tombs. His violent anti-social behavior had stirred fear and hostility in the local residents. When he met Jesus, he found one who loved him and accepted him just as he was. In that acceptance he found the faith to return from the world of unreality into which he had escaped to the real world of people and relationships. Jesus' love brought wholeness to his shattered life.

Another example of the unconditional acceptance of people as persons which characterize Jesus was his attitude toward those who crucified him. In the midst of excruciating physical and emotional torment, he prayed for his executioners to be forgiven. Then too, in the last moments of his life, he gave to one of the thieves crucified with him the assurance of God's forgiveness.

In the Gospel stories of those who met Jesus are some of the finest illustrations of the therapeutic power of love. Jesus was not primarily a healer. He had decided in wilderness not to win people by spectacular methods. Yet wherever he went, healings occurred. They were the natural consequence of love, for love is the life-force from which we come. Jesus, as no man who had lived before him, realized his own potential to love and lived in spiritual union with the Ultimate Creative Power of the Universe. The dynamic of love transformed casual contacts with people into significant confrontations; confrontations in which people found healing of body, mind, and soul. The miraculous healings attributed to Jesus were not cases of divine intervention in the laws of nature. They were, instead, manifestations of the proper use of God's basic law of human nature, the law of love. All that Jesus did that appears extraordinary, he was empowered to do by love. Anything that he did we can do also if we are willing to give ourselves in love. Loving opens our souls to the infinite resources of a loving God who longs to love the world through us.

No one can love like this, however, unless they are willing to pay the price. Love is not a free ride. "Love bears all things, believes all things, hopes all things, endures all things." I Corinthians 13:7 (RSV) It costs to love. Sometimes it costs dearly. The huge cost of loving is clearly evident in the life of Jesus.

He loved his home-town and the people in it. Their rejection of him hurt him deeply.

His heart went out in compassion to the crowds that followed him. He felt their anxiety, confusion, and desperation. He poured out his soul to them sharing with them the Gospel of love. He stated his message in simple terms that a child could understand using simple illustrations from the detailed life of the people. But would they listen? No! In utter frustration he charged that they had eyes but could not see; ears but could not hear. They followed him just as long as it seemed to accomplish their selfish purpose. If Jesus would improve their material or political lot, they were all for him. But they were not interested in personal improvement and spiritual growth. Knowing that their needs were basically spiritual and being unable to reach them made his heart ache.

Jesus cherished the religious tradition of his fathers. He recognized great values in the laws of Moses and in the proclamations of the Prophets. It grieved his spirit to see the distortions and perversions perpetrated by the Scribes and of the Pharisees of his day. In love, he lashed out against them calling them vipers and hypocrites, trying to shock them into an awareness of their errors and sins. He couldn't teach them either. Instead of re-examining their teachings and practices, they sought ways to destroy him.

He concentrated his efforts on a small circle of intimate friends.

They followed him, living with him, and working with him through the major part of his public ministry. If only they could learn the life of love, they could share it with others. Even here his success was quite limited. They were so slow to learn! They fought among themselves over who was the greatest. When the chips were down, every one of them deserted him because they feared for their own safety. With friends like them he needed no enemies!

The heartache of our Lord was clearly manifested during his final visit to Jerusalem. As he came to the place where he could overlook the city he said, "O Jerusalem, Jerusalem, which killest the prophets and stonest them that are sent unto thee; how often would I have gathered thy children together, as a hen doth gather her brood under her wings and ye would not! Behold your house is left unto you desolate." Luke 13:24 (KJV)

His "triumphal entry" into the city must have been an agonizing experience. He knew that when this crowd learned the nature of his kingdom they would turn on him in hostility and resentment.

His tender heart broke when those he loved, those who he had tried to save, renounced him and sentenced him to the ignominious death of a criminal. To top it all, one of his closest friends betrayed him to his enemies, and another disciple denied even knowing him on the night of his arrest.

Why? Why? What had he done to deserve such suffering? He had loved! He who loved the most, suffered the most! His suffering was not the will of God. He suffered because other people had not learned to love. They reacted to him out of their animal instinct for survival. It took the form of jealously, greed, bigotry and brutality. But who won and who lost in this encounter?

Does it pay to love? Did Jesus win or lose by choosing the path of love? Does it cost too much to love completely?

The cost of love is not even worthy of comparison with the accomplishment of love in the life of Jesus. Love enabled Jesus to live a life without fear. As the writer of the First Epistle of John explains, "There is no fear in love; but perfect love cast out fear . . . He that fears has not been made perfect in love." I John 4:18 (NKJV) Fear is part of our natural survival equipment but when one learns to love completely as Jesus did, irrational fear is no longer necessary.

His relationships with people were never influenced by apprehension or timidity. He reasoned with the doctors of the law at age twelve to their delight and amazement. He challenged the religious establishment of his day in spite of its political influence and power. When the religious leaders succeeded in arresting him and bringing him before them in trial, his quiet courage intensified their jealous anger. When he stood before Pilate, Jesus refused to consider the charges against him worthy of an answer. One author describes this encounter in the words of Pilate, "I felt as if Caesar had entered the Hall, a man greater than even Rome herself . . . I questioned Him and He would not answer. He only looked at me. And in His look was pity, as if it were He who was my governor and my judge." (Jesus, The Son of Man, by Kahlil Gibran, Alfred A. Knoff Publisher, N.Y. 1928) Pilate was accustomed to men cowering before him, pleading for mercy. This man not only was not afraid, he caused Pilate to feel uneasy and anxious. Pilate sent Jesus to Herod who could have saved him since Galilee was Herod's jurisdiction and Jesus' home. Herod wanted to see Jesus perform a miracle but Jesus ignored him. This angered Herod but deep down it stirred an intense feeling of guilt for his murder of John the Baptist. Jesus told his disciples once, "Do not be afraid of men." Matthew 10:31 (KJV)

The infinite resources of love enabled him to live out this teaching for all to see.

The power of love delivered Jesus from the fear of death. One Gospel account tells of Jesus and his disciples crossing the Sea of Galilee by boat. A sudden storm blew up and the disciples were frightened for their lives. Jesus was asleep in the back of the boat. The disciples woke him up and said, "Teacher, don't you care that we are about to die?" Luke 8:24 (TEV) Jesus is supposed to have said to the wind and waves, "Peace Be Still." But I agree with those who feel that it was to the disciples that he directed these words. He may have calmed their fears, not the wind and waves. When we call to mind the descriptions of the crucifixion, we see here not a trace of fear. He acknowledged the reality of pain and suffering by quoting from Psalm 22. "My God, My God, Why have you forsaken me? But when the end comes, in quiet confidence he commends his spirit to God.

So many people today are afraid to be alone. They shudder at the thought of isolation for any considerable period of time. They substitute a radio, recorded music, or TV, VCR, DVD for people, when they must be alone. There is no trace of such fear in Jesus. Instead, he insisted on having time alone. Love had made him appreciate himself and enabled him to find that communion with the spiritual realm that can only come when one is alone.

Because of love, Jesus escaped the disabling blight of inferiority feelings. Self-confidence is another consequence of mature love. Jesus had few, if any, doubts about himself. He knew from early childhood that he was a son of God. He lived his life in constant awareness of that fact. Those who heard him speak were impressed by the authority with which he spoke. It was not the authority of an organizer of religious tradition. It was the authority of a man who knew who he was. He did not hesitate to challenge the rules of the past. "You have heard that it was said, 'An eye for an eye, and a tooth for a tooth.' But now I tell you: do not take revenge on someone who does you wrong." Matthew 4:38,39 (TEV) He dared to challenge the rigid customs that concerned Sabbath activity and ceremonial cleansing. On whose authority? On his own authority as a son of God, and his call of God to declare Good News.

Love sharply heightened Jesus' sensitivity to life and the world around him. He knew more of the Life-source of the universe than any human being who preceded him. Accepting the love of God and giving himself in loving response gave him a clear and accurate insight into the nature of the Deity. Out of this insight grew his courage and his confidence. He lived moment by moment in the awareness that the creative ground of all that is, is Love. He drew upon the limitless resources of that love again and again in his ministry to needy people. In his hours alone he was revitalized and renewed by intimate fellowship with that ultimate source of love he called Father. In his teaching he shared with his disciples and with all who would listen, his personal knowledge of a God who is concerned, involved and available to all who open their lives to Him. Living the life of Love, Jesus was in tune with nature. He appreciated the glories of the world around him: the beauty of the lilies, the glory of the sunset and the blessing of rain. He saw God's truth revealed in nature and used it to illustrate some of his finest spiritual truths. He seemed to sense where the fishing was best and his disciples claim that on several occasions he walked on water. If these stories are true, he was able to do these things because he was so in tune with the loving source of nature that he knew and used principles such as the power of mind over matter which we are only now beginning to explore.

Most noticeably, love made Jesus sensitive to people and their needs. He could sense, beyond their words and their cover-ups, what their real needs were. When the man suffering from palsy was brought to him for healing, Jesus perceived that his real problem was guilt and he ministered to that need. When the rich young ruler came seeking salvation, Jesus discerned the root of his problem and said, "You still need to do one thing. Sell all you have and give the money to the poor, and you will have riches in heaven; then come and follow me." Matthew 19:21 (NRSV) Jesus saw in Peter the potential to be a great leader if only he could learn to love. He worked with him diligently and eventually he did become one of the outstanding leaders of the early church. On at least two occasions this super sensitivity helped Jesus recognize that people in a deep coma were not really dead as the people around them supposed. He saved them from being buried alive and restored them to their families. While traveling through Jericho on his last trip to Jerusalem, love caused Jesus to look up into the sycamore tree and see Zaccheaus. He saw him as a person in need crying out for help and he met that need that day. Zaccheaus was a new man with a new lease on life. (Luke 19:1-10)

The life of love that Jesus lived was an exciting life full of meaning and significance. Every day was another chapter in the adventure of helping people and making this world the kingdom of love and light. By loving he fulfilled his highest potential. Love is its own reward. The joy of loving far surpasses any suffering that love entails.

Love's finest compensation is the participation in eternal life which it affords. Eternal life is not a future state awarded to those who kept the rules in this life. It is a quality of life which is attained in the here and now by those who learn to love. "Whoever loves is a child of God and knows God." I John 4:8 (TEV) Whoever knows God has come into contact with the eternal and is participating in eternal life.

Jesus learned to love at a very early age. He lived in unbroken communion with the Love at the heart of the universe. All that he said and did had about it the quality of the eternal. He told his disciples, "I have overcome the world." The temporal and transitory had no power over him. The disciples heard and wondered but did not understand. The full impact of his words and his life was not clear to them until after his death. When Jesus was crucified and died as any other man, his friends naturally concluded that hate and violence and evil had destroyed him; that life was a hopeless lost cause. Imagine their surprise when he appeared to them after his death. The records of his appearances are too numerous to be ignored and their impact on his disciples is an obvious fact of history. His Love broke through the realm of the material to awaken their souls to the eternal. Now they believed that he had overcome the world. Love is at the heart of the universe. Those who dare to love, do participate in eternal life. Jesus had demonstrated that the life of love is the only way to live life fully.

In Jesus, the God who made us free creatures capable of love, got a winner. Jesus was the pioneer of a new and living way to God. He chartered the trail to abundant life. He was the first (qualitatively) of many brothers in God's family of love. He opened the door for us to participate in eternal life by teaching us to actualize our love potential.

Chapter VII
Eternal Life—Here and Now
A New Way to Live at Its Best

"As we send love energy to others, we become the channel for an energy that originates with the divine source and moves through us, like a cup filling and spilling over to others."
James Redfield (The Celestine Vision)

"Someday, after we have mastered the winds,
the waves, the tides and gravity, we will harness
for God the energies of love,
and then for the second time in the history of the
world, man will have discovered fire."
Pierre Teilhard DeChardin

"My sheep hear my voice,
...they follow me and I give them eternal life."
Jesus (John 10:27,28)

God's greatest winner, Jesus of Nazareth, taught us in word and example how to live life at its very best. Jesus said, "I have come in order that you might have life – life in all of its fullness." (John 10:10b TEV). What Jesus appears to be saying is, whoever believes my word and follows my example will participate in eternal life – in the here and now. By following the path of love, one becomes increasingly in harmony with the power of Love at the heart of the universe. One will participate in the life of the Divine – the community of Love.

Jesus knew who he was. He was God's special son on God's special mission to introduce all people to the God of Love and to enlist the willing as partners with God in creating a human society permeated by love and compassion. The religion of Jesus was not an other worldly religion where people are good so that they can be rewarded in some future life. His goal was to help people make the most of every day by being channels of God's love to every person they meet every day of their lives. In the first chapter of John's Gospel, it says that everyone who receives Jesus as their leader and commits themselves to walking the path of love are empowered to know who they are – they are sons and daughters of God – born of the Divine Spirit and participating in eternal life.

Love is more than a positive, pleasant emotion. It is a rational decision – an act of the will. God made a rational decision to create human beings in his likeness – free to exercise reason and capable of giving and receiving love.

Jesus describes a God worthy of our love and devotion. Jesus assures all people that God loves them and wants for them what is best. Jesus invites people to join him as partners with God in the adventure of creating a better world through the power of love. Jesus warns that this is not an easy task. There are risks of rejection, being misunderstood - even persecuted. In spite of all the challenges, it is the only way to live life in all of its fullness.

The first step in this new adventure is to make a commitment, as total a commitment as possible, to accept the God of Jesus, to follow the teaching and example of Jesus, and to seek out a community of fellow adventurers who worship the God of love, and to help God expand a loving social order.

This requires a new way of experiencing life and making decisions. We must have the courage to rise above our obsessions with ourselves and our own well-being. It is daring to lose ourselves in the adventure of love; to dare to believe that love is the ultimate law of life. It is a decision – an act of our free will, to be loving persons whatever the cost.

People make this commitment at different times, in different ways, under different circumstances, or in different places. Some children make this commitment gradually while growing up in a loving home, learning to believe in the God of Jesus, and to value the teachings of Jesus. They adopt for themselves this loving lifestyle. Others make this commitment at special events in their life - at the time of Baptism or joining the church. Others make this decision at a time of emergency. They cry out "O, God, get me out of this mess and I will follow Jesus!" Not everyone who makes this commitment actually follows through with it but a significant number do. Some people make this commitment out of desperation. Their life is falling apart around them and they feel as though they have nowhere to turn. In desperation, they turn to God and Jesus helps them transform their life.

The place where people decide to follow Jesus may be different. Some decide in a worship setting. Others may decide as a result of studying religion or the Bible. Occasionally, people decide to move in Love's way while meditating at a beautiful place in nature. They feel the Spirit of God and choose to walk in His way.

There are interesting stories of people who have decided to follow Jesus as a result of a vision or a dream. Place, time or circumstance are not as important as daring to follow through on the commitment. When people act on their commitment to walk the path of love with Jesus, they begin to experience the joy of loving, the wonder of contact with a higher plane and the encouraging presence of Jesus in their life.

The actual practice of walking with Jesus on the path of love is called, by the philosopher/theologian Soren Kierkgaard, a "leap of faith." It is daring to act on love whatever the cost! It is faithfully practicing the teaching of Jesus to "love your neighbor as you love yourself." (Matthew 19:19 TEV). This is risky business. There is no way of knowing how people will react. Some may reject the love that is offered. Some may try to take advantage of a kind loving person. Hopefully, most will respond in a positive appreciative manner. Jesus taught that our loving is not conditioned on the response of the other person. One does not love in order to get love in return. When one loves as Jesus did, one loves other people because they are human beings, made in the image of God and worthy of love. Our love for other people should be unconditional, whether they are good or bad; whether they accept our love or reject it. We love because we have committed ourselves to be loving persons modeling our lives after Jesus. Loving does not mean approving their bad behavior. Loving tries to show people better options that are less destructive. We believe that love is the ultimate power of the universe and the best way to live.

It is extremely difficult for people to perform this act of faith if they have never experienced love from another human being. The children who grow up in the atmosphere of love, experiencing love from their parents, will find it easier to believe in the God of love and will give themselves in love much more readily than persons deprived of love in their home. Children who have not felt love in their home, who have never experienced love from any significant person in their life, do not know what love is. They do not know God and will probably never know God unless somebody loves them. If they never experience significant love from another person, they are doomed to a miserable, lonely, frightful hell, all the days of their life. What this world needs, more than anything else are more lovers. When we give ourselves in love as Jesus did, it benefits both us and those we love. In loving relationships, the God of love we committed to believing in, becomes a living reality; a dynamic force that inspires us and challenges us to keep on loving. Through our loving, this God comes alive in the lives of those we love.

Having made this sincere beginning on the path of love, all life is seen in a new perspective. We look at life and people through the eyes of love. We see the loneliness, fear, and unhappiness of the people around us. This is a sight we had been blind to because we had had eyes only for ourselves. Our hearts go out to them in compassion and concern. We try to help them by affirming their accomplishments and long to help them to even greater fulfillment.

Love causes us to see people as persons, not as things. We relate to them as significant individuals. We do not use them as means to arrive at our ends. We do not manipulate them in order to satisfy our desires. Love wrecks the walls of isolation, fear, and bigotry that separate people from one another. It enables us to see all people as family. In the light of love, each day is a fascinating opportunity for new and deeper relationships with people. To the extent that these relationships are characterized by compassion and concern, they become a factor of the eternal. Each relationship is an opportunity to know more of God and to make God more of a reality in the lives of others.

If we would follow Jesus, the pioneer of our Faith, on the path of love, we must learn to hear. How accurate was Jesus' description of most people when he said, "They listen, but they do not hear or understand." (Matthew 13:13) This power of selective hearing was demonstrated to me quite noticeably on one occasion. I gave a lecture to a group of high school young people on the subject, "Jesus and the New Morality." Sometime later when my wife was teaching the same group in a Sunday School class, this subject came up. She was shocked at what they quoted me as saying. They had missed the basic emphasis of the lecture. They had heard only what they wanted to hear. They listened but did not hear or understand. This is not the way of love! When we recognize people as significant persons and enter into meaningful relationships with them, we make a conscious effort to hear them and to try to understand. When they feel loved and accepted by us, they will reveal more of themselves to us. They will share their feelings, their hopes and aspirations, and their problems with us. Often we will not know what to say. Fortunately, we usually don't need to say very much, just listen, love, and understand. Having a significant person with whom we can openly share life is a miracle working therapy. It frees us from the prison of lonely isolation. It makes it possible for us to know ourselves better and to see life and its problems clearer. Good listeners are desperately needed. As agents of the God of Love, we should be responsive to this need.

Love endows us with a sixth sense that lets us heed the message and feeling behind the words. Words are frequently only a polite cover up for intense feelings of hostility, inferiority, or anxiety. The insensitive person will be fooled by the words. He will listen but not understand. Understanding and unconditional acceptance make cover ups less and less necessary. People can dare to be their real selves and the energies wasted in concealment can be channeled into more positive directions. In the atmosphere of love, one can verbalize attitude and sentiments which have never been expressed, but may have been a source of guilt or anxiety for a long time. Getting out their feelings in the setting of unconditional acceptance can free a person from their grip and power. Jesus calls us as individuals and groups to this compassionate ministry of listening.

Commitment to love helps us grow toward maturity. It is not enough just to respect others and listen to them acceptingly. Love leads us to share ourselves with them as well. Jesus shared himself openly and honestly with his disciples. He revealed his thoughts, his ambitions and his faith to them. Peter, James, and John were with him during one of his important conferences with people of the sprit realm. At the time, they were not prepared for an experience of contact with people from a higher plane. Yet this is what they observed on the Mount of Transfiguration. It was, however, an important part of Jesus' life and he shared it with them.

This sort of openness is not easy for us. We have to work at it. Bitter experience has taught us to be careful of what we say because anything we say may be used against us. This is a characteristic of life on the animal level. In the jungle we reveal as little of ourselves as possible. But in the green pastures of love, things should be different. As we learn to love, we begin to take down the protective walls behind which we have been hiding our real selves. We open up and share ourselves more fully with those we love and our love grows to a deeper and deeper level. Yes, occasionally we'll get hurt. Still the end result makes insignificant the minor hurts along the way. By sharing ourselves in love, we begin to live life on a different plane. We take our place as sons and daughters of God. We sense a spiritual tie to all who have walked this way before us. We live life enthusiastically and make the most of every day. As we love our way into greater harmony with God, and become more intimate friends with Jesus, we move towards the fullness of life that God intends for us.

If we look to Jesus as the supreme example on the way of love, we see a man of action. Jesus was not content to preach beautiful sermons about love. He lived love. He would have agreed wholeheartedly with the writer of the Epistle of John who said, "My children! Our love should not be just words and talk; it must be true love which shows itself in action." (I John 3:18 TEV) From the moment that we awake until we again seek the restoration of sleep, we should be looking for ways to love. Our greeting to the first person we see in the morning can be an act of love that starts them on a good day. If the intimate associations in the home are ordered by love, our homes become pockets of heaven instead of chambers of hell. If in our chosen occupations we cultivate the opportunities for loving, the day's work becomes a sacred calling. The people we meet come alive as significant persons. We will discover more to do in the name of love than we have time or energy to do. What we do accomplish will be far more than we ever dreamed possible. The doing of it will fill our lives with joy. We will be too busy to indulge in self-pity, too involved to be bored, too engrossed in the present to worry about the future. We will make the most of life as it comes to us. We will live every moment to the fullest. Some years ago a song was popular in the Country and Western field entitled, "I want to Live Fast, Love Hard and Die Young." When we walk with Jesus on the path of love, we will live fast, love hard, and never die! We are participants in eternal life. We are citizens of heaven, a heaven God helps us create right here in this life.

Love becomes the ethic of our lives. It is the guideline by which we determine right from wrong; that which serves the cause of love; that which lifts persons to fuller and better life - that is right! That which degrades persons and reduces them to the level of animals or things - that is wrong!

This ethic is not as simplistic as it may sound. The simple way is to have a rule book that spells everything out in black and white. This is the way of legalism. But legalism rarely serves the needs of people. It sets "obedience to the rules" as the highest good. Jesus rebelled against this type of legalism in his day. "The Sabbath was made for man, not man for the Sabbath," he insisted. Man's fulfillment, man's well-being, this is the highest good. This means that all rules, all customs, and all social practices have to be evaluated by what they do to persons. To the extent that they contribute to health and development they are to be honored and preserved. But when they have outlived their usefulness, when they become ends in themselves, when they limit man's potential for growth, they must go.

The love ethic is totally relativistic. It judges every action by what effect it has on persons. This places the responsibility on the individual to consider every act carefully. There are no blanket rules, no easy answers. Each deed must be evaluated in light of its short term and its long term effects on people.

This approach to the situations of daily life requires the scrupulous use of our intellectual abilities. As Professor Joseph Fletcher put it in his book, *Situation Ethics*, "Love uses its Head". In making our decisions, we calculate the possible effect of our action on us, on those directly and immediately involved, and on others more remotely influenced by this decision. This is the struggle that Jesus experienced, in the Garden of Gethsemane. He knew that he had pushed the religious establishment to the breaking point; that if he stayed in Jerusalem it would cost him his life He knew that he could run to the hills of Galilee and be relatively safe for some time. He had to decide if it would be best to stay in the main stream of public life, stand for his principles and pay the price exacted, or would it be better to continue his teaching to a small group in some wilderness hideaway. He was not sure which would be best. He agonized; he sweat blood over this decision. He considered the alternative results to him. He wondered which decision would be best for his disciples. They understood so poorly his teaching. Perhaps they needed more training. He thought of the multitudes there in Jerusalem and the multitudes who would come after them. He talked to his Father to try to confirm the most loving decision. He decided to stay with the people, to stay in the midst of things whatever the cost to himself and the risk to his disciples.

History has proven his decision a right one! In his death upon the cross, and his resurrection, the depth of his love and the truth of his teachings were indelibly stamped on the heart and conscience of his followers. His appearance to them from another plane after his death confirmed his message that those who invest themselves in love are participating in eternal life on this plane of existence or on a higher one.

Love is the demanding ethic by which we choose to live. It steers a course between the easy extremes of rigid legalism and irresponsible lawlessness. The individual must stand on his own two feet and decide. He can't shift his responsibility to a written list of "do's" and don'ts." Neither can he coast his way through life doing only what he feels like doing, following the way of least resistance. There is no room in love for the "I don't care" or the "I'll do it tomorrow" attitudes! Love demands that we make the best, the most creative decision possible when the time for decision has come. This is not the ethic possible for the selfish, the cowardly, or the faint hearted. The ethic of Love is most difficult when there are no good options or when all options are negative. Love demands that all options in such a situation be considered. Then one must choose the action that does the least harm. This is the ethic by which the sons and daughters of God fulfill his highest potential and move toward the realization of the Kingdom of God here on earth.

Where do the traditional acts of piety fit into this new way of living pioneered for us by Jesus? What of prayer, worship, and the spiritual disciplines of fasting and study?

Jesus was a man of prayer. His disciples recognized prayer as a key factor in the power and success of his life. Before he entered his public ministry, he spent forty days in meditation and prayer. A night of prayer preceded his choice of men who would be his special disciples. He often arose early in the morning for prayer. He would leave the multitudes and retire to a place of solitude for days at a time. We have very few of the prayers of Jesus recorded in the gospel but the prayer which he taught his disciples give us some insight into the nature of his prayers. He recognized the existence of a purposeful reality he called Father who was the ground source of all that is, who is experienced in relationship with other people, who leads us to life abundant if we will listen and accept His way.

This is quite different from much that is called prayer by some would-be pious people today. For many, prayer is a monologue in which we tell God things he needs to know, and instruct him on how to run the people and the world around us. Prayer is a verbal device by which we twist the arm of God and make him do things for us that he wouldn't have done had we not prayed. By prayer we can control the weather, manipulate the people around us, and get anything done that we want done as long as we add to our prayer the magical words, "in Jesus name." If God does not respond to our demands, we repeat them over and over, louder and louder. If he still pays no attention, we get two or three others to join us in the same request. Then God has to grant it because the Bible says so. We will remind Him of what the Bible says if He hesitates, just in case He forgot.

This is not the way that Jesus prayed and it is not the pattern of prayer for those who would walk with Jesus on the path of love.

Prayer should be a conscious awareness of the Love from which we come. This creative dynamic force is within us and around us. He seeks to lead us to fulfillment, to the development of our highest potential, to the experience of love in relationship with those who share life's journey with us. God is with us constantly doing for us all that love can do. We distance ourselves from Him with our fears, our worries, and our self-centeredness. Prayer is the overcoming of that alienation, the "tuning in" to the Ground of our Being. It is the quiet realization of the force of Love that sustains us. It is the courage to be sons and daughters of God. To believe that in Him no ultimate harm can damage us and to know that death, for us, is a minor transition from eternal life here to eternal life on a higher plane.

Jesus lived in a constant awareness of that Presence. His whole life was a prayer. Prayer was a way of living. That is why he could say, "Pray without ceasing." When he withdrew for prayer it was not to find God, but to think through a problem and sharpen his sensitivity to his Father who was always with him.

Following Jesus, we must learn to live our lives in an ever-increasing consciousness of that Creative Dynamic within us and around us. We begin to perceive His reality in the loving relationship we enjoy with others. We sense our "in tuneness" while we are doing the deeds of love. In the quiet moments when we wrestle with life's problems, make important decisions, or plan out another day's activities, if we are open, we can feel the surge of the Deep from which we come. Our finite capabilities are inspired to unexpected accomplishment by this contact with the infinite. Prayer becomes a way of life. It is a way of loving with the best of our human resources expanded and enriched by our growing communion with God. It is practicing sensitivity to

God and to our fellow human beings. It is participating in the Life of the Divine – it is experiencing eternal life in the here and now.

Worship, like prayer, can be a boon to living the life of love. It must be understood in love's perspective if it is to be truly beneficial.

Worship is not something that God demands because he is so holy and we are so sinful. It is not groveling in the dust before some celestial potentate whose ego must be boosted by our proclamations of praise and adoration. It is not a magical ritual by which we win the favor and assistance of a begrudging Deity.

Worship is a special effort to "tune in" to the Ground of our Being - to commune with the God from whom we spring. We should live in a continual awareness of God, but we don't. Worship is our effort to tear down the barriers and remove the obstacles that keep us from knowing fellowship with God. Through worship we seek to learn how to live more fully the life of love. We use worship aids to sharpen our sensitivity and to improve our understanding. The worship experience may be private or shared as a part of a group.

Corporate worship is enriched by employing a number of worship aids. The architecture of the building can help focus one's attention on God and His love. The organ music and then anthems of the choir inspire the spiritual. The group participation is singing, and other parts of the service may improve our God consciousness. To know that we are not alone in our quest makes it more meaningful. The order of the service, the color and drama of the ritual will hopefully contribute to a higher spiritual awareness. The instructional elements of the service are designed to stimulate our thoughts and lead us to greater truth about life and people and love. The purpose of the service is to equip us to live more fully, and to make life more meaningful for those around us.

Private worship seeks to accomplish the same purpose. The worship aids are different. We choose a location and a time that helps us focus in on God. We may use music. We may light candles or follow a certain ritual of prayers or readings. The method of private worship will vary according to individual preference and differing personal backgrounds. The results are what are important.

Creative worship, public and private, will contribute to creative living. It improves our sense of unity with the Love out of which we come, and inspires us to live love in our daily relationships with people.

Properly understood, the spiritual discipline of fasting can be an asset in the Christian life. It must not be used as a means to impress people with our piety. It is not a punishment we inflict upon ourselves for lack of spirituality. It is a living reminder to us of Jesus' instruction that man should not live by bread alone. It is a physical means of calling our attention away from the physical to the spiritual. It accomplishes this by reminding us of who we are. We are the sons and daughters of God. We are in control of the physical and it is not in control of us. This greatly improves our self-image and improves our usefulness to God in accomplishing his purposes.

Study is a vital discipline in this "new and living way." We study to learn the truth about life and love and the world. We need to be open to truth from many sources. The modern sciences of psychology and psychiatry can teach us much about people and how to relate to them lovingly. Philosophy can help us work out a consistent life based on love. A study of Sociology can assist us in building a loving society. Other sciences and technologies can enable us to make the very most of this good life which we enjoy. Theology, our understanding of God, integrates the important knowledge we receive from all these fields and help us develop into the whole person that God intends us to be.

Jesus, our Leader and Friend, was the pioneer and perfector of the path of Love that enables us to participate in eternal life and makes us channels of God's love to the world. If we follow him to the best of our ability, we will grow in our harmony with God, and our awareness of Jesus as a present friend and guide to life – toward life at its best!

Chapter VIII
Rational Christians and the Bible

> *"Like the earlier paradigm, the emerging paradigm sees the Bible as sacred scripture, but not as a divine product. It is sacred in its status and function but not in its origin."*
>
> Marcus Borg (The Heart of Christianity)

For centuries, millions of people have sought answers in the Bible to life's most difficult questions. It has become the best selling book in the world. *"Within its pages are words from God that can help you understand yourself, make important decisions, gain peace, renew hope, and experience God's love."* (ZondervanBibles.com)

Surveys have shown that over 90% of Americans own at least one Bible. Sales records show that at least 20 million Bibles are currently sold each year in the United States in addition to millions of Bibles that are distributed free.
(Bible Facts – Saintmathewschurches.com)

IT IS CLEAR THAT THE BIBLE HAS BEEN ONE OF THE MOST influential books in the development of Western Culture. Many of the moral principles of our culture reflect the influence of the Bible. The Ten Commandments, the Golden Rule, and other social teachings from the Bible have influenced our laws and practices.

The Bible, like religion, can have both positive and negative effects on human behavior. The Bible has been used, at various times, to justify such negative activities as slavery, racism, war, discrimination, and violence. But for thousands of people, the Bible has been a source of inspiration and spiritual guidance that has empowered them to live positive lives of loving service that has made our world a better place.

Reading the Bible has been and can be a life-transforming experience. The Gideon's mission is to place Bibles in various locations such as hotel rooms, hospital rooms, military settings, malls and prisons where people can have access to them. They believe that the Spirit of God will move people to pick up a Bible and read it. If you have ever heard a Gideon present their ministry to a church group, they tell of sick people in a hospital reading the Bible and finding strength and help in a time of need. They tell of people in hotels who were down and almost out to the point of even considering suicide, who in desperation started reading the Bible and found new hope and went on to live productive lives. The Bible is not a book of magic, but reading it can open one to an experience of God's love.

While the Bible may be a "best seller," it is not the most widely read book in our time. Christianity is often called a religion of "The Book", but the reality is that most persons who identify themselves as Christians, even active Christians, have only sketchy ideas about the contents of the Bible. Most people are satisfied to let their clergy tell them what they need to know. This means that their knowledge of the Bible is filtered through the theological and doctrinal orientation of their clergy and the Christian group which they represent.

The theological and doctrinal views of Christians concerning the Bible vary a great deal. For the American Unitarian Christian,

"The Bible, while inspired by God, is written by humans and thereof subject to human error." (www.americanunitarians.org)

The fundamentalist Christians have a rigid absolutist approach to the Bible. When one conservative scholar was asked, "Why should a person study the Bible?", his answer was that it is the only Authoritative Word of the living God to man! It is a Divine Revelation! It is God – breathed literature! It is the only infallible rule of faith and practice. It is the only infallible guide to salvation!" (biblicalstudies.org) If one believes this way, it means that every word of the Bible is written by the finger of God and is literally correct. In a recent Gallup poll, 35% of Americans believe that the Bible is the literal inerrant word of the Creator of the universe.

A more moderate approach would be to say that the Bible is Sacred Scripture; that the writers were inspired by God and that God is gradually revealing himself to the human family and teaching how he wants us to live. Dr. Robert Schuller reflects this more moderate view in his introduction to the "Positive Thinkers Bible" (NKJV) (pg. VIII). He suggests that we should not turn the Bible into a text book on science. "Scientists can tell us much more about geology, genetics, or astronomy than the Scriptures do. Do not make the mistake of trying to turn it into a chronological account of humanity on planet earth. Look for the deeper truths that transcend such shallow presumptions. The deeper truths are that God loves you – and that we should love each other, too."

The Bible is a library of sixty-six books credited to forty different authors and reflecting a broad panorama of history, law, culture and customs. It was composed over a period of about 1,000 years, starting with Moses about 1200 B.C.E. and concluding with the latest writings in the New Testament about 200 C.E. Some stories in the Bible were probably told around campfires or early homes as much as 2000 years before they were written into the narratives of the Bible. The Creation story (especially the Adam and Eve story), the Tower of Babel story, the great flood story, and other stories have parallels in the myths of other ancient Middle East peoples.

The Bible contains a variety of literary styles. The narratives, as mentioned; law, history, prophecy, wisdom literature (Psalms, Proverbs, Song of Songs, Ecclesiastes and Job), and some apocalypse are part of the Old Testament. In the New Testament there are Gospels, Epistles, and Apocalypse. All of these writings were written for religious purposes and all have a theological "spin" to their presentation. The spin is different in different books at different times.

For Christians, the Bible is considered sacred scripture. Now what does that mean? Historically it means that a group of theologians and Bishops in the fourth and fifth Century of this current era (C.E.) decided which books would be included in the Bible and therefore considered Sacred Scripture. They accepted the Jewish list of books for the Old Testament. The Jewish leaders had established their list of accepted books in the latter part of the first century with general agreement by the early second century (C.E.). The books of the New Testament were written over about a 100-year period from 50 C.E – 150 C.E. The books that made it into the Bible were the books most widely used and appreciated by early Christians. By the fourth century, the powerful leaders of the Church, those that developed the Nicean Creed, had defined what true Christians should believe and by listing the correct book of the New Testament they defined what Christians should accept as Sacred Scripture. They called themselves "Orthodox" and declared that their teachings were the exact beliefs of Jesus and his Apostles. Most Christians have blindly accepted these exaggerations and distortions ever since!

Another reason the Bible is considered Sacred Scripture is that throughout all of Christian History, these Sacred Scriptures have been read and sung in worship as an instrument for worshipers to experience the Divine Spirit during worship. The fact that this spiritual experience does occur sometimes in worship has reinforced this practice. If participants in worship would listen to scripture meditatively and ask themselves, "Is there any Divine message for me in this scripture presentation?" worship might be a much more exciting experience for them.

Reading and studying the Bible in private meditation can make the Bible sacred for the reader when they hear a Divine message to them. If you have read the entire Bible, you know that this is not a frequent experience. But it does happen and when it does, it is an awesome and sometimes a life-changing experience.

Conservative Christians, who believe that every word in the Bible was dictated by God to the writer, see every word as sacred directives that must be believed and followed. To do this, they disengage their rationality and blindly accept on FAITH that every word is literally correct and must be followed. It is probably good that most of these Christians don't read the Bible completely. As mentioned, the Bible does in places, order genocide against the enemies of God. Consider what could happen if a Fundamentalist Christian father happens to read as his devotional scripture one morning, God's instruction about faithfulness to God alone in Deuteronomy 13:7-11. It says that if your brother, your wife or one of your children comes to you and entices you to try a new religion – to worship a different God, you are to kill that person immediately! At breakfast, his son tells him that his new girlfriend is a Buddhist. He has been studying that religion and he plans to become a Buddhist and he thinks his father should check it out. Now the father has a dilemma. Should he act like a rational civilized human being or should he obey God and terminate his son? Most fundamentalists will find some excuse to not take the Bible literally, but some fanatics may do exactly what God commands. That may sound extreme, but in 2005, that is exactly what suicide bombers have been doing in Iraq, in Israel and in London. They take literally the instructions of the Koran, "True believers fight for the cause of God but infidels (all non-believers) fight for the devil. Fight then against the friends of Satan.... Say 'Trifling are the pleasures of this life, the thereafter is better for those who would keep from evil." (Koran 4:74-78)

Fanatics in any religion are dangerous. Literal interpretations of Holy Scriptures are often the reason or the excuse for barbarous behavior.

So how should a rational Christian approach the Bible? A rational Christian who accepts, as a working hypothesis, that God is Love and the clearest revelation of this God is in the life and teachings of Jesus will evaluate and interpret the entire Bible through the theology of Love and with keen historical and cultural perspective. As an example, the early writers of the Old Testament believed in many gods; they were convinced that their God was the best and most powerful. Yahweh, their God, had chosen the people of Israel as his people. He loved them and blessed them as long as they worshipped him properly. If they failed to worship properly, he withheld his blessing and protection. Their God had no positive feelings for any other people. Other people were only considered favorably if they were subjugated to the people of Israel. Knowing this helps one understand the genocidal directions of God against Israel's enemies in several places in the Old Testament.

When the evangelist Paul writes his letters to the Churches telling women to be silent in church, be subject to husbands, do not have short hair and men not to have long hair, this is not direction from God, but the reflection of the cultures in which he was raised and some reaction to the libertine Hellenistic culture of his time. Yet many people today in conservative churches feel that they are obligated to follow these instructions as directives from God!

When a rational Christian reads the Bible meditatively, and an idea pops into the mind, that idea is evaluated by the theology of Love before it is acted upon. Does this idea inspire a loving response? Would acting on this idea make the world a kinder, better and happier place? If the answers are positive, then act upon it! If not, ignore it! Acting on positive, loving ideas brings us into greater harmony with God, and makes the world a better place.

A rational Christian who identifies Jesus as the highest expression of the God of Love should read the Gospels of the New Testament over and over again to be fully aware of what Jesus did and said! The other New Testament writings are useful in so far as they are in tune with the God of Love and the teaching practices of Jesus. When you read the other New Testament writings and even as you read the Gospel, it is important to remember that within a few years of Jesus' death, the focus of his followers shifted from practicing the religion of Jesus to a new religion about Jesus. This is most clear in the writings of Paul. For Paul, all that was important about Jesus was that he was a descendant of King David; was born of a woman, died on the cross, was resurrected and now sits on the right hand of God in heaven. In all of his writings in the New Testament, Paul says almost nothing about the life and teachings of Jesus. The source of Paul's Christian Gospel were revelations that came to him in desert settings. Yet the surprising truth, affirmed by several scholars is that Christianity, as it is taught and practiced today, is really Paulineism, a religion using the name of Jesus, created by a man who never met Jesus and never tried to learn anything about his life and teachings.

The Gospels are our most reliable source of information about the life and teachings of Jesus. Even here, we need to remember that the earliest gospel, the gospel of Mark was written 40 years after the events described and the latest Gospel, the gospel of John was written 60 to 70 years after the events. Clearly even the Gospels reflect the influence of early church reflections about Jesus. Therefore even the Gospels must be scrutinized in light of the theology of Love.

In conclusion, the Bible is a great book; an influential Book and serious Christians should read it to know what is in it. Rational Christians will read the Bible through the filtering lenses of a theology of Love. The Bible is our best source of information about the life and teachings of Jesus. There are other Gospels that are available for reading. They are interesting, but most of them were written in the second century or even later. That means 100-200 years after the events described.

I repeat, a rational Christian accepts that God is love as a working hypothesis and that the life and teaching of Jesus shows us how to enter into harmony with God. Based on that premise, they will be diligent students of the Gospels and they will have a working knowledge of what is in the rest of the Bible. A rational Christian is suspicious of all absolutes. When any person says their religion is absolutely correct and all others are false, a rational Christian knows that he is listening to either a fool or a fanatic. Both of these are dangerous especially if they get into a position of power and influence.

Another challenge in the 21st Century of this current era is how do people of different religions relate to each other. This is really challenging when most of the major religious groups on our planet are committed to the idea that their religion is the only right religion for everybody. Even with Christianity, how can Christians work together when many feel that their version of Christianity is the only correct one?

This will be addressed in the next chapter.

Chapter IX
Christian Tolerance of Other Religions

> *"Religions are correctly judged by their impact on their members. Any religion that motivates its members to be kinder, better and more loving is good religion! A religion that motivates arrogance, negativity, hate and violence is bad religion."*
>
> GOE

CHRISTIAN TOLERANCE OF, OR RESPECT FOR OTHER Religions is virtually an ox-moron, a total contradiction in terms. Christians have a hard time respecting different groups of Christians. Each Christian Denomination, either overtly or covertly, thinks that their understanding of Christianity is the only right approach.

Tolerance for other religions is a challenge that is forced upon us by living in the 21st century on planet Earth, which has become a Global Village. The combination of modern communications and ease of travel means that we are inevitably confronted with other religions. Living in the United States, where freedom of religion is one of our basic rights, we live with and work with people from a variety of religious backgrounds. In any good-sized city, we will find Catholic Christians, Orthodox Christians, Protestant Christians and many participants of other religions, Buddhists, Hindus, Sikhs, Moslems, Jews and a number of people practicing different spiritual paths. In the United States we respect the right of all persons to practice their religion of choice so long as their practice of that religion does not endanger the safety and welfare of other citizens. Like it or not, the fact is that we live in a religiously pluralistic society.

Tolerance of other religions does not mean that we assume that all religions are absolutely true. It is clear the different religions make certain claims that logically contradict each other. Tolerance is respecting the fact that all religions represent the attempt of human beings to explain ultimate Spiritual Reality and to design a method for human beings to enter into harmony with that reality.

One of the greatest difficulties with religious tolerance is the absolutist claims and goals of various religions. Radical Jewish groups see as the ultimate goal the rebuilding of God's Temple on Temple Mount in Jerusalem and all peoples honoring and worshipping the God of Israel. The ultimate goal of radical Christians is expressed by St. Paul in his letter to the Philippians where he says "at the name of Jesus every knee shall bow; of those in heaven, and those on earth, and of those under the earth, and that every tongue shall confess that Jesus Christ is Lord." The ultimate goal of radical Moslems is that all peoples will be ruled by Islamic law and all infidels will give proper worship to Allah or be destroyed.

In Jewish, Moslem and Christian religions, there is emphasis on End-Times. All are concerned that God is going to bring an end to time as we know it and force all people into compliance with His Will. Each of these three religions knows that God is going to end things in their favor. These end-time ideas are called Apocalypse, and are expressions of a violent, angry God, a God not worthy of worship by intelligent human beings.

It is most startling to find rational non-religious thinkers talking about Apocalypse. M. Rees in his book *Our Final Hour*, and Sam Harris in his book *The End of Faith,* both predict an Apocalypse within the next century. They predict the fall of civilization when religious fanatics and wars of religion, cause our biggest bombs to fall on our biggest cities in defense of our religious differences. Religious fanatics are more than willing to meet their maker, but if we don't act quickly in the name of reason, they may drag everyone else with them to meet their maker. These are secular authors who are agnostic at least but they recognize the extreme danger of fanatical religion.

Religious leaders of the various religions of the world recognize the dangers of extremism, absolutism and terrorism in the name of Religion. The first congress of Leaders of World and Traditional Religions met in September of 2003 in Astana, Republic of Kazakhstan, to explore how religions can work together to promote understanding and cooperate in actions to improve the quality of life for the whole human family. One of their concerns was terrorism and violence in the name of religion. The Alaska Bahai'i' Community in a recent conference indicated that the 20th Century has compelled the people of the world to begin seeing themselves as members of one human family and the earth as our common home land. According to their internet website, the world Interfaith Congress represents the Major World Religions working together to build a better world.

At a world Forum of religious leaders representing over six recognized world religions, Professor Hamid Bin Al-Refale, president of the International Islamic Forum for Dialogue in Saudi Arabia called on all Muslims and non-Moslems to work together for peace affirming that cultural and religious diversity should encourage a real co-existence among human societies. Rev. Yasumi Herose of Oomato, Japan affirmed that "However

different our rituals, doctrines and interpretations, all religions have the same ideal…that is a world full of love and mercy, a place where people find comfort, safety and peace." (Brief excerpt of the keynote address).
(www.omoto.or.jp/forum/angle/billreport.html)(retrieved August 2005)

At the 2004 meeting of the Parliament of the World's Religions, it was pointed out that politicians, business leaders, and other leaders in society recognize that there is a moral and spiritual dimension to the great problems that afflict our world society. One of these is overcoming violence, especially when it is religiously motivated or targeted. Inter-faith cooperation and understanding could help accomplish these goals. (www.cpwr.org/2004parliament/news/opinionbraybrooke.htm) (retrieved August 2004)

His Holiness Tenzin Gyatso, the Fourteenth Dalai Lama in an articled called "A Human Approach to World Peace," identifies four principles for achieving world peace: (1) universal humanitarianism is essential; (2) compassion is the pillar of world peace; (3) all world religions are already for world peace in this way as are all humanitarians of whatever ideology; and (4) each individual has a universal responsibility to shape institutions to serve human needs. He says about religion, that all world religions have similar ideals of love, the same goal of benefiting humanity through spiritual practice and the same effect of making their followers into better people. All religions agree upon the necessity to control the undisciplined mind that harbors selfishness and other roots of trouble. Each religion teaches a path leading to a spiritual state that is peaceful, disciplined, ethical and wise… Humanity needs all the world's religions to suit the way of life, diverse spiritual needs, and inherited national traditions of indvidual human beings.

(www.tibet.dk/iarmapa trust/religion.htm) (retrieved August 2005).

What a wonderful thought about cooperation in world religions. These ideas are great, but they are accepted by only those moderate and liberal expressions of the world religions, especially Christianity and Islam. As we noted earlier, the fundamental extreme right of both of these religions have a history of absolutism and violence. They have ambitions of world domination.

Words are beautiful but action is necessary. The moderate leaders of World Religions must find a way to discredit and discourage the fundamentalist extremists. Moderate Moslem leaders have been reluctant to condemn the extremists and declare that their behavior violates the principles of the Faith. Christian leaders must also be quick to condemn extreme behavior by fundamentalist Christians.

Political leaders often avoid getting involved in religious matters. This is a luxury they can no longer afford. The preaching of hate and violence must be against the law and violators should be jailed.

A rational Christian's response to other religions is practical and compassionate. Every human being is a person of worth who is free to choose the religion that is best for him. If their religion makes them kinder, better, happier, and more productive, it is good religion, whatever name is used. If it makes them meaner, hateful, violent and destructive, it is bad religion, whatever the name. One should be compassionate toward those who practice bad religion. People who practice "bad religion" are often victims of cultural traditions, family expectations, fear of dire consequences if they question their religion, or deluded by nebulous hopes of great rewards in the next life.

However, being compassionate toward these persons does not mean excusing their bad behavior. Violent destructive behavior can never be excused on the grounds of religion. Persons who practice such behavior must be corrected or isolated to protect the privilege of other people to be kind, caring and productive. While freedom of religion is a high social value in America, the government should not hesitate to act decisively against any person or group who practices or promotes violent destructive behavior in the name of religion.

Rational Christians are open to, even seek, positive dialogue with people of other religious persuasions. They practice the art of active listening. They try to set aside preconceived notions and hear these persons' ideas about the ultimate issues of life. When the other person is open to hearing their views, they share their ideas, not as absolutes, but as their working hypothesis on the nature of reality.

I had the high privilege to participate in this type of dialogue some years ago. I was attending a Clergy Continuing Educational event at a Seminary in Washington D.C. The Seminary ran out of dorm space for the students in this event. I was given a room in a dorm at American University. The person I shared the room with was a young man from Saudi Arabia. He was attending a special class at the University. When he learned that I was attending the Seminary, he engaged me in a dialogue about religion. The only Christians he had met previously were extreme fundamentalists. He was intrigued to learn about a more moderate approach to Christianity. We talked late into the night for the five days we were together. His background was a moderate version of Islam. I can't remember what class I was attending at the Seminary, but I will never forget the positive enlightening dialogues I shared with this young man from Saudi Arabia. When my class was over, we separated as spiritual brothers who, even though we used a different name for God, were brothers in the common task of making the world a better place. We had developed a deep respect for one another and a spiritual bond that rose above our different religious traditions.

Christians can dialogue with people of other religions more meaningfully when they focus on the life and teachings of Jesus and less emphasis on Pauline theology and the Creeds of early Christianity. The God of Jesus, he called, "Heavenly Father" and this Father loved all of his children. Rational Christianity does not claim to be the only path to a knowledge of God. Love is the measure of any religion. If it teaches love and inspires its members to be kinder and more compassionate, it is good religion.

There seems to be a movement within Christianity to focus on God as love and a renewed emphasis on the person and message of Jesus. Pope Benedict XVI on his first Encyclical focuses on God as Love. In the opening paragraph he quotes I John 4:16 where it says "God is love, and he who abides in love abides in God." The Pope indicates that these words express the heart of the Christian faith. His prayer at the end of the Encyclical is a "back to Jesus prayer". "Show us Jesus. Lead us to him. Teach us to know and love him, so that we too can become capable of true love and be fountains of living water in the midst of a thirsty world". This focus of God as love and renewed interest in life and teachings of Jesus will inspire more Christians to engage in dialogue with people of other religions.

Rational Christians are not the only Christians trying to refocus Christianity to its true core – the life, teachings and spirit of Jesus. In 1985 a group of committed Biblical scholars formed the

Jesus Seminar. Their mission was a new assessment of the Gospels of the New Testament using historical and textural research to get as close to the true words of Jesus as possible. They recognized that the earliest Gospel was written forty years after the events described. The latest Gospel written is dated somewhere in the last fifteen years of the 1st Century by most scholars. It was written as much as 60 or 70 years after the events described. They recognized that over the long period before the Gospels were written, the early Christian Church may well have put words in the mouth of Jesus that supported their particular interpretation of what Jesus should have said. This is a sincere attempt by serious scholars to help regular Christians who study the Gospels to recognize that some of the words of Jesus very likely were deleted or exaggerated before they were written down in one of the Gospels.

Another example of modern refocusing on the life teaching and spirit of Jesus as a practical guide for living is the Books of Joshua series written by Joseph Gerzone. Father Gerzone was an active parish priest for many years in a number of different settings. In 1981, his cardiologist told him that if he continued his typical work in the parish, he would be dead in a year. The doctor encouraged him to retire. He retired and started writing. His first best seller book was Joshua. This is a fictional story about a young man who comes to a small town and works as a carpenter. Father Gerzone projects how Joshua (Jesus) would live out his message of love in our modern settings. Other books with the same theme are: Joshua in the City; Joshua and the Children; and Joshua in the Holy Land, to mention a few. Helping people imagine how Jesus would behave in a modern setting must have been a healing activity for Father Gerzone. He retired in 1981. The book Joshua came out in 1983 and, very soon became a best seller. He has been writing and lecturing in various settings ever since. His latest book, Joshua in a Troubled World, was copyrighted in 2005. Fr. Gerzone was initially surprised about the broad interest in Joshua. In his book, A Portrait of Jesus, he says "People have a hunger for Jesus and for a genuine understanding of what His Good News really is, whether they are Christians, Jews, Hindus, Buddhists, or even those who cannot identify with any faith." (pg. Image Books 1998) Joshua's God is a loving Heavenly Father who loves every human being, wants what is best for all his children, forgives their errors easily, and actively wishes to engage in a relationship with each person to help them find joy and fulfillment. What God expects of his children is that they appreciate the good world he has made for them; accept his love for them, find joy and happiness in loving the people around them; and become God's partners in the great task of creating a human society based on love, peace, and positive productivity. They are called to help the needy, befriend those persons who feel isolated, and expose those who are using their freedom destructively. Joshua's God respects human freedom and feels pain when they misuse their freedom because he knows that it is going to hurt them and hurt the people around them.

In conclusion, rational Christians affirm the worth of every human being. They respect the freedom of every person to choose their own religion. They welcome opportunities to dialogue with persons of other religious traditions. They enthusiastically work together with people of all religions who value love and are working to create a more peaceful, compassionate human family. Rational Christians expose and reject any religion that is motivated by hate, and uses religion as an excuse for violence, greed, or domination.

Chapter X
Dealing with End-Time Hysteria

"Imagine failures of reasonableness so total that our largest bombs finally fall upon our largest cities in defense of our religious differences."
Sam Harris (The End of Faith)

END TIME HYSTERIA HAS BEEN A PROBLEM IN CHRISTIANITY since its beginnings. The books most popular among the common people in Jesus' day were The Book of Daniel, The Book of Ezekiel and The Book of Enoch. These are technically called apocalyptic literature. This type of literature is very popular when people are oppressed and hoping for some Divine intervention. The earliest followers of Jesus were looking for a Messiah – a person empowered by God to deliver the people from oppression. The disciples became convinced that Jesus was the Messiah so they followed him through thick and thin. When they entered Jerusalem, on that first Palm Sunday, they fully expected Jesus to declare himself as the Messiah, and then, with Divined intervention, He would drive the Romans out of Palestine (at least). The plan was to set up the Messiah to rule the world. The disciples had an ambition to set on Twelve thrones and rule over the Twelve tribes of Israel (see Matthew 19:28). With Divine help, they believed that Jesus was initiating the end of the age. Jesus had gone to great effort to teach them about God's kingdom of love but it just could not get through their end-time hysteria. Jesus told them plainly that his preaching had created enemies and those enemies would conspire to kill him. (Matthew 16:21-25) Peter even tried to correct Jesus on this matter.

The disciples were devastated when Jesus was arrested one evening and executed the next day! Their End-Time hopes were unfulfilled! When, two days later, they were told by some of the women followers that Jesus' tomb was empty, they were excited but skeptical. Later when Jesus appeared to them on several occasions, he sent them forth to teach the entire world his message - that God is a loving heavenly Father and he wants all of his children to live together in peace and love. But his disciples could not give up the End-Time thinking. They created a second coming of Jesus as a new end-time. This time, Jesus would come with his holy army from heaven and force all peoples to follow him or be eliminated. The early Christians believed this so strongly that they lived in constant expectation of his imminent return. The Apostle Paul believed this more strongly than other Christians. It was reflected in his behavioral guidelines in his letters to the churches. He encouraged people not to marry, unless it was absolutely necessary, because Christ may return before they could start a family. People in one of his churches were so convinced that they stopped working and just sat around waiting for the end. In his second letter he told them not to be idle but that every person should keep working until the end time, second coming, occurs. He says that if a member does not work, he shall not participate in the shared meals. (See I and II Thessalonians). It is in the first letter to the Thessalonians that Paul describes the "rapture." When the Christ returns, the dead in Christ shall arise to meet Christ in the air and those of us still alive will rise after them to meet the Christ in the air and spend eternity with him and all the saints. (I Thessalonians 4:16-18). Many of the End-Time books of the "Left Behind" series, so popular in the latter part of the 20th Century and the early 21st Century, are based on this Scripture passage.

From the time of Paul until the present, Christians have been expecting this event to happen very soon. Over the centuries the End Time Hysteria has been most intense at special times: end of centuries, end of millennium (10th Century, 20th Century), and times of disasters or major wars.

One of the severest persecutions of early Christians, Empire wide, was during the last half of the third Century. Two great literary figures of this time escaped persecution, and wrote prolifically about this period. Lactantius wrote in Latin and Eusebius, Bishop of Caesarea, wrote in Greek. Lactantius was schooled in philosophy and wrote treaties in defense of Christianity. Eusebius is often known as the "Father of Church History." Much of what we know about the early centuries of Christianity comes from his pen. Both men wrote during the great empire-wide persecution period. Both men predicted the imminent return of the Christ by the end of the Third Century or early in the Fourth Century. Both men were wrong! What really happened early in the Fourth Century was Constantine (324 CE). The persecution ended and Christianity was affirmed. By the end of the Fourth Century (about 380 CE) Christianity was made the official religion on the Roman Empire. Now that Christianity was an acceptable religion, even a preferred religion, the emphasis on the imminent return of Jesus was not a strong focus of Christian teaching. A few charismatic preachers would predict the End-Time and gather a group of followers to join them in being ready for the Second Coming. When it did not happen as predicted, the credibility of the preacher was questioned and the groups fell apart.

End-Time Hysteria was high around the year 1,000 in Europe. Several would-be prophets predicted the End of the Age and gathered a group of followers around. When it did not happen, these groups also fell apart.

One internet site, in an article on end-time predictions lists as many as twenty-one predictions in the tenth century and thirty-five predictions of end-time events in the eleventh century. These are based on documents and historical information. Here are a few samples. The preaching of Aelfric and Wulfistan in England (10th century) warning of the last judgment indicated that the Anti-Christ would be released in the year 1000 and the Last Judgment would come soon after that. This was a theme in Christian preaching several places in Europe just prior to 1000. It was widely believed that Jesus would return on January 1, 1000. The significance of this date was that it was 1000 years after the birth of Jesus. People were on their best behavior; they sold worldly goods and gave to the poor; and swarms of pilgrims headed to Jerusalem to meet Jesus there. This was significant wide spread end-time hysteria in Europe.. A terrible famine in parts of Europe in the early 1000's convinced many that the end was near. The year 1033 was identified because it was 1000 years after the death of Jesus. Many pilgrims went to Jerusalem for this event. (Retrieved 9/23/05 – www.bible.ca/pre-date-setters.htm)

The list goes on and on. The focus on the date 1000 years after the birth of Jesus and on 1033 after his crucifixion was a great appeal among the common people. What we know today is that Jesus was probably born somewhere between 4 and 6 BCE. Herod the Great, who is part of the birth story in Matthew, died in 4 BCE according to Roman historical records. If Matthew's Gospel is accurate, then Jesus would have been crucified somewhere between 27-29 CE.

In the years 1524-1526, Muntzer, a leader of German peasants had a vision in which God told him that if he and his followers would "destroy the high and the mighty," then the Lord would return. God also promised that his followers could catch the cannon balls of the enemy in their sleeves and not be harmed. He and his group armed themselves and attacked the government forces and were mowed down by cannon fire.

In a 1995 letter about prophecy sent to the mailing list of RENOVARE' (8 Inverness Drive East, Suite 102, Englewood, CO 80112-5609), Richard J. Foster lists a number of people who predicted the end time. A reformer, Hans Hut claimed the Christ would return on Pentecost, 1528. He gathered 144,000 saints to join him in preparing for this event. It did not happen and the movement disintegrated. The famous evangelist in colonial American, Jonathan Edwards, won many converts by his prediction of the imminent return of Christ. In the nineteenth Century, it was Charles Finney who won converts with similar themes. William Miller, a student of Bible prophecy, predicted that Christ would return in 1843. When it did not happen, he recalculated the year to be October 22, 1844. His followers, called the Millerites, sold their property and goods and joined William Miller in various hills in up-state New York waiting for the end. It is estimated that 40-100 thousand people were involved. When it did not happen, the people returned to their normal lives, a little bit wiser.

These are just a few historical examples of the multitude of prophets of doom who are able to convince gullible people to follow them. These are examples of sincerely misguided leaders who were trying to help people avoid disaster. There have been a number of prophets with less honorable goals. Some of these collected the people's money and when the event fizzled, the leader was no where to be found.

The most recent upsurge of End-Time Hysteria occurred at the end of the 20th Century. During the late 1990's, end-time hysteria was flooding the book store and magazines with the promise of doom and disaster. Some of these authors like Dr.

Tim LaHaye had learned from history. Instead of predicting events and dates for the end, they wrote fiction stories describing their concept of the end times. That was a smart move because if it did not happen as described; they could say that the stories were fiction. Others protected their predictions by setting a range of time. Rev. Jerry Falwell in 1999 proclaimed that Jesus would return within the next 10 years. Many others follow the same old pattern of exact predictions. Stuart Cobbs claims that the "Rapture of the Church" will occur in October of 2005. John Dutchman predicts that the earth will be hit by several comets beginning in August 2009. Michael Drosnin predicts atomic holocaust and world war in 2006. These are samples of dire predictions with even more available. (retrieved September 16, 2005 from www.religioustolerance. Org.)

Joseph Girzone, author of the books about Joshua, demonstrates his opinion about the end-time. He has Joshua speaking with a group of sincere Christians worried about the end of the age. Joshua says, "The world will not end until my Father's entire plan is accomplished. His creation is still in the process of evolving perfection, as all things are gathered into His Son. When all things are made perfect in His Son, then the work of creation is accomplished and not before." (Joshua the Home Coming, Image Books, Doubleday, New York, November 1999, pg. 162).

A rational Christian living by the working hypothesis that God is a loving Heavenly Father who cares about each of his children rejects the God described in the Book of Revelations, the Book of Daniel and all such apocalyptic literature. The ranting and raving of all violent end time predictors are equally rejected as totally out of character with the life and teachings of Jesus. If the God who created human beings free and capable of loving, chooses to end the world as this literature describes, he would be admitting his own failure in his most adventurous experiment of creation. Love never fails. God has all the time needed to perfect a human family who chooses to live by love. In Jesus, God calls each of us to become more loving, so that our fellowship with him is more joyous and we influence society to be more loving.

At their core, most of the major religions of the world call on all people to treat all other people as they themselves would like to be treated. Many of the great Philosophers affirm the same idea. Love is the answer and in due time it will triumph.

For Christians, the resurrection of Jesus and our experience of his spirit with us is God's promise that love never fails.

Chapter XI
Dissonance in Christianity

It is not enough to possess virtue,
as if it were an art; it should be practiced."
Cicero

"Paul has been called by many names ... Some say
as compliment or indictment (wrong either way),
that he was the actual founder of Christianity."
John Crossan and Jonathan Reed (In Search of Paul)

OVER MANY YEARS OF EXPERIENCE AS AN AGENT OF Organized Christianity and in the study of religion and philosophy, I have become increasingly aware of significant dissonance or incongruity.

To an independent observer, when a person claimed to be a Christian, the observer would expect that such a person followed the teaching of Jesus Christ and modeled his life after the example of Jesus. The reality is that most Christians know very little about the teachings and examples of Jesus and even less about what is contained in the Bible as a whole.

The major reason for this is that within ten years of the death of Jesus, his followers shifted their focus from the teaching of Jesus to a religion about Jesus.

This is demonstrated clearly by the earliest writing of the New Testament in the bible. The earliest writings were the letters of Paul to churches he had established in Asia Minor (currently Turkey and Greece). Thirteen of the books of the N.T. are letters of Paul addressing the needs and concerns of these Churches. In all of these letters, Paul quotes the words of Jesus a maximum of only three times, saying nothing about the facts of Jesus' life other than birth, death and resurrection. Paul's letters were written in the late 40's or 50's of the first century. Paul was at first a persecutor of Christianity, but after a special spiritual experience, he became one of the greatest missionary – evangelists. He saw his mission as a missionary to the gentiles.

The four Gospels of the New Testament were written 10 to 40 years after the letters of Paul. As the first generation of Christian leaders were dying or being executed, several Christian communities felt a need to write down the acts and teachings of Jesus so that future generations would know what Jesus did and what he taught while he lived among them. Since these Gospels were the product of different Christian communities, they represent four somewhat different stories of the life of Jesus. In them we learn what Jesus believed about God – what Jesus taught about how people should live so that they would please God and know God as their heavenly Father who loved them.

Over the centuries that followed, the letters of Paul became the primary source for Christian theology rather than the Gospels. To this day, Christianity is defined much more strongly by the theology of Paul than by the religion of Jesus. There are some very odd incongruities in this. Some scholars consider Paul the founder of Christianity, as we know it.

First, Paul calls himself an Apostle of Jesus in almost all of his writings. The fact is that Paul never met the historical Jesus during his lifetime. Amazingly, he claims in his own writings that he made no effort to learn about the historical Jesus from the Apostles who followed Jesus during his earthly ministry. His knowledge of Jesus and his theological insights came to him in visions. In his letters, he even claims to be a superior Apostle – a greater Apostle than the people who were eye-witnesses to the deeds of Jesus, who personally heard his teachings and witnessed his death and resurrection.

The second major incongruity between the theology of Paul and the religion of Jesus is the fundamental issue about the nature of God. For Jesus, God is a loving heavenly Father who cares about all of his children. God respects human freedom but gladly forgives any person who recognizes that he is living improperly and wants to turn around (repent) and start in the right direction. This is clearest in two parables of Jesus in Luke Chapter 15 – the lost sheep, and the lost son.

For Paul, the primary quality of God is holiness. This holy God has decreed that any person who sins must die! Paul says that all human beings have sinned and are subject to death. God is incapable of forgiving until he has a perfect human sacrifice, who is willing to die for the sins of the whole human family. For Paul, Jesus was that human sacrifice which empowered the holy God to forgive anybody who asks for forgiveness in the name of Jesus. Since Jesus was that perfect, willing human sacrifice, God raised him from the dead and elevated him to the right hand of God. Jesus is coming soon by the power of God to accept all his followers and force all other people to live as God directs. (The reign of God.) Paul was convinced that this would happen very soon even in his life time.

The difference in these two concepts of God is catastrophic. What is even more amazing is that most Christians do not begin to recognize these differences. This is because they have been taught to read the Gospels through the lenses of "Pauline Theology". Most people just don't realize the extent to which Christianity has come to be defined by Paul's theology.

In my last parish, I was teaching a Bible study class and suggested to them that modern Christianity is really more Paulineism than the religion that Jesus taught. Some in the class challenged this idea, so I engaged the class in research. In our city, the Saturday newspaper included the sermon title and scripture text along with the name of the churches. I proposed to the class that they survey the next Saturday paper and list how many of the Sunday sermons were going to be based on the teachings of Paul from his letters, and how many would be based on the teachings of Jesus from one of the Gospels. At the next class session, they reported that about 90% of the sermons were based on the writings of Saint Paul.

When I was the Minister of Education at a large church in Colorado Springs, the Senior Minister and I invited the congregation to a Dialogue between the ministers on the question "Who is the true founder of Christianity as we know it – Jesus or Paul?" It was an interesting dialogue and the meeting room was filled with over one hundred people. I prepared a hand out to help people be aware of the dissonance between the theology of Paul and the teachings of Jesus. The hand-out proposes a hypothetical conversation between the three Persons of the Trinity of traditional Christianity. The discussion is about the creation of human beings – should they be free – how should their sinfulness be addressed, how can the Reign of God be accomplished, and how could they participate in eternal life.

DIVINE DIALOGUE - HUMAN BEINGS AND SALVATION
PAUL'S PLAN VS. JESUS' PLAN

Picture with me a conversation that took place in the celestial realm at some time before Creation. The discussion is between God, the pre-existent Christ, and the Holy Sprit.

(Content of the first proposed plan is based on the writings of Paul)

God: (To Christ) I want to create a universe. On the planet Earth we will create human beings. We will give them the freedom to choose between right and wrong. They will be fruitful and fill the Earth with human beings. Adam and Eve will choose to disobey me. You know that because of my righteousness I cannot tolerate such sin. I decree that the soul that sinneth shall die. I decree physical and spiritual death on Adam and Eve. The stain of their sin will be inherited by their children. All human beings will be sinful from the day they are born and will be under my sentence of death. (Romans 1:25; I Cor. 15:22; Rom. 5:12, 17; Rom. 6:23)

Christ: But Father, it seems such a waste to have all these human beings die just because of the sin of Adam and Eve.

God: I agree, Son, but because of my righteousness, I have no choice. I do want to save a few of them. I have already selected them to be my sons and your brothers. (Rom: 8:29) But, in order to do this, I need help from both you and the Holy Spirit. To satisfy my anger against sin, somebody has to die. It has to be somebody who does not already deserve to die. You, Son, are the only possible candidate. You could take on the human form by being born of a woman, then die in the place of al sinful persons. I would resurrect you and you could return to our heavenly fellowship here. (Gal. 4:4)

Christ: I am willing to leave our fellowship, take the human form, die for human sins so that their sin can be forgiven and they can be in right relationship with us. (Phil. 2:7) This will satisfy your anger and demonstrate your love. Salvation will be our free gift to humanity. (Rom 5:6-11) If I die, I want it to be for all human beings. If Adam's sin condemned all people, I want my sacrifice to save al persons. (Rom 5:12-18; I Cor. 15:22, 45)

God: No, I don't want to save them all, only a few, my elect. (Rom 8:28-30) I will have mercy on whoever I will and I will destroy whoever I will, because I am God. (Rom 9:14)

Christ: But Father, how can you blame people for resisting or disobeying you when you compelled them to do so?

God: I am God! They are in no position to question me. Can the clay ask the potter, "Why have you made me this way?" I made a few to be saved and to Hell with the rest. I am God - I do as I please. (Rom. 9:19-24) As a matter of fact, my willingness to save a few, with your help, is a clear demonstration of my great love, righteousness, and justice.

Christ: But Father, how are we going to select the few that are to be saved?

God: We must make sure that the action is totally ours so that none of those miserable creatures have anything to boast about. We will make faith the necessary requirement for receiving salvation. Since sinful humans are not capable of faith, this is a task for you, Holy Spirit. You put faith in the hearts of those who have been selected for salvation, then they will be saved by grace through faith which is not of themselves. It will be purely a gift from God for which they have done nothing, and therefore cannot boast. (Eph. 2:8; Rom. 5:15; Rom. 3:23-25)

Spirit: I will be glad to do my part in salvation. But how do I force free persons to accept faith, if they don't choose to accept it? If they do choose to accept, they could boast about making right choices.

God: Just tell them the choice was made for them before they were born and they should just be grateful. You have another task, also. These humans are so stupid and inferior that even after being selected for salvation, they cannot pray with any intelligence. I want you, Holy Spirit, to dwell in them, and when they come out with those unintelligible mumblings, you pray for them because I can understand you. (Rom 8:26-27)

Spirit: I can do that.

Christ: Will we really be able to fellowship with these inferiors?

God: It will take some effort. You and the Spirit will have to totally take over their personalities and direct their thought and activities in the ways of purity. Actually, they cease to live and we live in and through them. (Phil 1:21; Gal. 2:20; II Cor. 5:15; Rom. 8:14-17; Rom. 8:11; Rom 6:5-11; I Thes. 5:23)

Christ & Spirit: We can do that, but it seems like such a waste of effort.

Christ: Father, let me review your plan and see if I understand it. You make a universe, put free human beings on it. They sin almost immediately. Your wrath is kindled against them and all future generations who inherit their sin. Still, you want to save some of them. You want me to go to Earth, be born of a woman, and then die as the victim of your wrath - as a substitute for the few you want to save. Then you require faith in order to save these few, so you want the Spirit to put faith in their hearts so all action is our action. You just can't stand the thought that one of those humans might boast for making a right decision on his own. You want the Spirit and I to live in these people and direct their lives so that, in the end, they will be acceptable to us. Is that right?

God: You got it – that is my plan!

Christ: I don't want to hurt your feelings, but I think a good God could come up with a better plan!

God: Do you have a better idea?

(End of Paul's Plan)

*****

JESUS' PLAN

Christ: Yes, let's call this "The Jesus Plan". We make the universe, put human beings on Earth, and give them freedom. We make them little less than we are – in our own image. We allow ourselves the ability to forgive sins upon request because our nature is to love. The Spirit and I will try to guide human beings to fulfill their divine potential to be loving persons and create a loving society. We will try to show them that their sins are really self-destructive. We are opposed to sin because it hurts them. We will speak to them through nature.

We will call out prophets and leaders, who listen to us better than most, and let them also speak for us to the people. We will keep looking for a person willing to fully listen to us and fulfill his ultimate potential. We will find one. He will be Jesus (that is why we call this "The Jesus Plan"). He will be fully open to our guidance and I will be fully incarnated in him so that forever he and I will be inseparable. He will be the Son of God (my influence) and Son of Man, or Ultimate Human being (his accomplishment, because of openness to us).

He will teach people about us and about themselves – their worth and divine potential. He will teach them how to love more fully that they may be one with us in the activity of love. Arrogant representatives of organized religion will not like Jesus and his message. They will be motivated by selfishness, pride, prejudice, greed, political expediency, religious fanaticism, and other sins, to try to destroy him. He will warn the men and women who follow him that changing this sinful world into the Kingdom of Love is not easy but it is God's (Our) will. Sinful men will kill him – the best, kindest, most loving – dies because of people's sins. Hopefully, this will demonstrate to all people the dreadful results of sin and will challenge people to turn from their sins and learn how to love.

After they crucify Jesus and bury him, we will, on the third day, resurrect him so that all may know that his teachings and his example is what we expect of every person. This is the way to be all you can be, to live life well, and to enjoy fellowship with us and eternal life. We (Christ and the Spirit) will guide and empower his followers to change the world and make it the kind of place we intended it to be. We will work with humans as a team of equals. We will enjoy fellowship with them. They will enjoy participating in our family of Divine Love. They will be glad to have learned how to use freedom creatively. They will no longer fear death because they are already participating in Eternal Life! This, Father, is "The Jesus Plan." I think it is far superior to the previous plan we considered.
Spirit: I agree! I would much rather work on "The Jesus Plan."

God: SO BE IT!

Some Biblical references in support of the Jesus plan: Gen. 1:27-31; Psalm 8:1-9; Proverbs 8:22-31; Isaiah 2:2-4; Matthew 5-7 (Sermon on the Mount); Luke 15; John 1:1-18; John 10:7-18; I John 3:11-18;, 4:7-12.

The first plan considered in this divine dialogue is based on the Theology of Paul. Each element is annotated with the exact reference to a letter of Paul by chapter and verse. This is to facilitate people checking for themselves about the theology of Paul.

The second proposed plan reflects that positive message about God and the human family that started in the first chapter of Genesis and reappears frequently through out the Bible. It is clearest in the Gospels. It presumes that God is Love, that human beings are made in the image of God, given freedom and the potential for loving God, themselves, and loving other people as they love themselves. The path to a positive relationship with God is the path of love – taught and demonstrated by Jesus. The ultimate fulfillment of God's plan will be realized when the whole human family learns that love is the answer – the ultimate human value.

Remember that I am not claiming that such a conversation did occur or even could occur. This is a purely hypothetical dialogue designed to highlight the dissonance between the teachings of Paul and those of Jesus.

Traditional Christianity has favored strongly "The Paul Plan" occasionally adding elements of "The Jesus Plan." This mixture creates a discordant theology. The real issue is the nature of God. My principle is, "Never worship a God who is not at least as good and loving as you are!"

Therefore, I choose to resolve the dissonance between the theology of Paul and the teaching of Jesus by rejecting the Pauline theology and accepting, for me, a God of Love, who respects human freedom, and values every human being - a God who invites human beings into "one-ness" with him in the great adventure of creating a human society dominated by love, peace, and harmony within the human family and harmony with the natural world.

This is clearly a matter of free choice by a rational person who chooses to worship a God who is better, kinder and more loving than any human being and in his love invites us into progressive union with him in the adventure of loving. A right relationship with God is achieved by right choices, right action, and right openness to the Spirit of Love revealed in Jesus.

Chapter XII

Foundational Disciplines and Considerations

He is forever free who has broken
Out of the ego-cage of I and mine
To be united with the Lord of Love.
This is the supreme state. Attain thou this
And pass from death to immortality."

Shi Krishna in the Bhagauad Gita.
(a meditation of Ganthi)

THIS UNIQUE APPROACH TO CHRISTIANITY IS STRONGLY influenced by the disciplines of philosophy, history, psychology and theology.

Philosophy: All philosophical systems are carefully reasoned out and designed to minimize internal inconsistency. They establish a frame of reference through which the world and its inhabitants are understood. This is a rational construction, a paradigm which guides one's actions in the world.

Most philosophers, from Socrates and Confucius to Immanuel Kant, have a humanistic ethic that insists that a person should treat other persons in the way they would like to be treated. Kant's categorical imperative "act only on that maxim which you at the same time will to be a universal law." What this means is that people are to be respected as ends in themselves and never used for the selfish interest of another.

Philosophers are skeptical of any person who claims to have absolute truth, especially religious leaders who claim absolute truth based on their Scriptures or their visions from God or some other Divine representative. This skepticism is greatest when the source of absolute truth contains blatant internal inconsistencies. The class example of this is those Fundamentalist Christians who claim that the Bible is the Word of God – is absolutely true in every verse. Another example can be seen in those Christian leaders who claim that the Creeds of the second through the fourth centuries express the exact teaching of Jesus and the earliest Apostles. This is a claim which, subject to any logical analysis, would be found to be untrue. Yet this is the belief of most Christians today.

The nature of human freedom is a hotly debated issue in the disciplines of Philosophy, Psychology and Religion. Deterministic psychologists insist that freedom is an illusion – that our actions and responses are determined by our genetic inheritance and our social conditioning. Humanistic psychologists insist that the ability to reason makes human beings free to make choices that impact themselves and others. One's rational choices have a significant impact on one's future!

Philosophical determination denies the power of free choice and insists that every action is a response to a cause and similar causes will regularly produce similar effects. The divergent view, in the 16th Century is clear in the writings of Erasmus, a contemporary of Luther and Calvin. Erasmus insisted that human beings had free will – they were capable of reason which enabled them to make choices and nobody could predict, with certainty, what choice they would make – not even God.

The traditional view of most Christians has been that human beings are incapable of free choice. They are genetically flawed by "Original Sin" and cannot make good choices without assistance by God. John Calvin believed that human beings are "totally depraved." Calvin and Luther promoted the idea that free choice was impossible because all events and responses were predestined by God. Their views reflect the teaching of St. Paul and St. Augustine. This is part of the negative Biblical teachings about humanity. But some Christians choose to accept the positive Biblical view that humans are created in the image of God and empowered by God with reason, freedom and the potential to be loving. The Rational Paradigm here-in appreciates the views of the humanistic psychology and the philosophy of Eramus.

One philosophical system, popular in the early Christian period was Stoicism. Many Stoic philosophers combined the ideas of determinism and free choice in the same system. The Stoics believed that the events of life were pre-destined by a Higher Power but that every person was totally free to choose how he would respond to these life events. In the late half of the 20th Century, Viktor Frankl, a survivor of Nazi death camp, in his book *Man's Search for Meaning,* says "Everything can be taken from a man but the last of the human freedoms – to choose one's attitude in any given set of circumstances, to choose one's way." (pg. 104)

Christians who commit to the hypothesis that God is Love and that God is committed to human freedom as a prerequisite to being able to love, share views similar to the Stoics. They recognize that many events in life are beyond our control. The random acts of nature – storms, earthquakes and such are beyond one's individual control. The people around us are free to choose positive or negative behavior. When people choose to misuse their freedom, it can impact negatively in our lives. In every situation of life, we have a rational choice about our response. One may choose to react to negative situations with more negative behavior. On the other hand, one can consider what is the most loving response to this situation and choose that response. That is what Jesus is reported as doing. Choosing a loving response brings us closer to God and empowers one to make the most of bad situations and to celebrate with joy the good experiences of life.

Approaching life with a Rational Christian Paradigm enables one to face negative events without guilt and fear. Nothing negative comes from God. Most of the evil in the world is because people misuse their freedom. Accidents and natural disasters are the random events that are beyond our control – not punishment from an angry God. In all that happens to us, God is with us empowering us to partner with him in transforming society into a kinder, more loving human family.

Psychology: The modern psychologists who most influence this rational approach to Christianity are Viktor Frankl (1905-1997) and Erich Fromm (1900-1980).

Viktor Frankl was a Jewish Austrian psychiatrist who was interned in Nazi death camps during World War II. He lost his wife and family but he survived. He observed that those prisoners who had a sense of meaning for their lives, survived better than those who gave up to despair. In the book, Man's Search for Meaning, Frankl shares some of his experience in the death camps and describes the treatment method he developed –

logotherapy. Logotherapy is striving to find meaning in one's life as the primary force. "What matters, therefore, is not the meaning of life in general, but rather the specific meaning of a person's life at a given moment." (pg. 171) "It did not matter what we expected of life, but rather what life expected from us. We need to stop asking about the meaning of life, and instead think of ourselves as those who were being questioned by life – daily and hourly. Life ultimately means taking the responsibility to find the right answers to its problems and to fulfill the tasks which it constantly sets for each individual." (p. 122) The right answer to life, according to Frankl, is love. He says that the salvation of the human family is through love and in love. One finds meaning in their life in three ways: by doing deeds of love, by experiencing love, and by suffering in the cause of love. For him, love is the ultimate and the highest goal to which man can aspire.

Erich Fromm was considered by many as a social psychiatrist. He was engaged in not only treating individuals but also addressing society. His analysis of society is that too many people operate on what he calls "The having orientation – that is that they define themselves by what they have. These people never have enough and are always afraid that they will lose what they have.

The positive orientation is the "being orientation" which expresses itself in loving, caring and giving. Being is living life with the excitement of loving and being productive – making a positive contribution to life. In his book, *The Art of Loving,* Fromm says, "Love is not primarily a relationship to a specific person; it is an attitude, an *orientation of character* which determines the relatedness of a person to the world as a whole." (pg. 36) He explains that the most fundamental kind of love, which underlies all types of love is *brotherly love.* "By this I mean the sense of responsibility, care, respect, knowledge of any other human being, the wish to further his life....Brotherly love is love for all human beings." (pg. 37)

Fromm asserts that "unconditional love corresponds to one of the deepest longings, not only of the child, but of every human being; on the other hand, to be loved because of one's merit, because one deserves it, always leaves doubt; maybe I did not please the person whom I want to love me, maybe this, or that – there is always a fear that love could disappear. Furthermore, "deserved" love easily leaves a bitter feeling that one is not loved for oneself, that one is loved only because one pleases, that one is, in the last analysis, not loved at all but "used."

In his book, *The Same Society*, Fromm explains "Love is union with somebody, or something outside oneself under the condition of retaining the separateness and integrity of one's own self." (pg. 37).

Clearly rational Christianity as described here is rooted in the existential psychology of Vicktor Frankl and in the social psychiatric analysis of Erich Fromm. Both men would agree that loving is the highest activity of human beings and that the salvation of the human family is in learning and practicing the art of loving instead of the art of war. Love is the ultimate value.

History: This rational approach to Christianity takes history seriously. It is interesting to identify where secular historians confirm or question the events described in the Bible. The story of the Hebrew people being slaves in Egypt for hundreds of years is not substantiated in Egyptian historical documents. The substantial contents of the first five books of the Bible, often called the Books of Moses, were passed to future generations as oral tradition for hundreds of years. The first four books took some written form about 1000 BCE, plus or minus 100 years. It is very likely that the book of Deuteronomy was written in the seventh century BCE, while Josiah was King of Judah. So while Moses may have been the original source, there would have been significant changes before it took written form.

Historically we owe a great debt to the writers of the four Gospels of the New Testament. Almost all that we know about Jesus is in those Gospels. There are only three or four slight references to a Jewish revolutionary being executed by Rome in the twenties or thirties of the first Century in Jerusalem. There was very little reference to Jesus in either Jewish or Roman history.

One should read the Gospels diligently, always remembering that in the decades between the events and the writing of the Gospels there may have been some embellishment. It is also useful to consider the target audiences each of the Gospels addresses. Each of the Gospels has their own theological bias. Rational Christians admit that they read the gospels through the theological bias of believing that God is Love, and Jesus exemplifies this in actions and in teachings. Rational Christians admit that the history of Christianity is frequently marred by a lot of un-Christian behavior.

From the beginning, different communities of Christians had their own understanding of who Jesus was and what was the primary focus of his teachings. While Christianity was subject to persecution in the first three centuries, there was not a lot of sharing and dialogue. Differences were dealt with by each group going its own way. When the Emperor Constantine made Christianity legal and even the preferred religion in the Empire, he insisted on some uniformity in Christian Doctrine. The Bishops of all major cities in the Empire were called to a Council at Nicea for the purpose of defining correct Christian Belief. The Council produced the Nicean Creed in 325 CE. Christian groups who did not agree with the creed were declared heretics and expelled from the church. Over the next 1000-1400 years as the church gained more power, there were barbarous atrocities within the Church - the crusades, the inquisition, genocide against entire communities that resisted the church. Significant numbers of church leaders were corrupt morally and politically. The Crusaders were promised that if they were killed in battle, they would go straight to heaven and avoid purgatory. The corruption that launched the Protestant Reformation was the selling of indulgences – that is you could be forgiven for some sin before doing it so that you could enjoy it without fear of punishment. This was "creative financing" to enable the Pope to build St. Peter's Cathedral in Rome. An example of blatant immorality had to do with John Hus, an enthusiastic preacher in Bohemia. Hus preached about the need for reform in the Church. He became very popular and had strong influence in that area of Europe. He was invited to the Church Council of Constance (1415 CE) to present his vision on reform to a selected group of Bishops. He was guaranteed personal safety by representatives of the Pope. When he arrived at the Council, instead of listening to his ideas, they tried him for heracy and burned him at the stake.

It was the success of the Protestant Reformation that drove the Roman Church to serious change in what was called the Counter Reformation.

There are too many atrocities in Christian History to address, but these are examples. A detailed study of this subject would be shocking to most Christians.

There are some very outstanding examples of positive Christian thought action demonstrated in the lives of Saint Augustine, Saint Benedict, Saint Francis, John Wycliffe, Martin Luther and

John Wesley to name a few. These focused attention on God's love and forgiveness. One of these who took most seriously the life and teachings of Jesus was Saint Francis of Assisi (1182-1226 CE). Saint Francis was as a young man a rich "party boy." He stopped in to an empty church to mediate and he heard Jesus speak to him from the cross and say "Build my Church." Francis rejected his riches and from that time tried to faithfully model his life after Jesus. His modeling of Jesus inspired many, even thousands, to join the Franciscan Order. They continue, to this day, ministering in the name of Jesus, following the example of St. Francis.

Theology: The theological foundation for rational Christianity began with Anselm of Canterbury (1033-1109CE). He developed a theology that affirmed the goodness of God, that God's intent for human beings was "beatific intimacy with God." All human beings had the capability for rationality which made them free to make choices and able to love God and other human beings. A human being's highest vocation is to strive into God with all of his powers – reason as well as emotion and will. In essence what this means is that God is love and our highest vocation is to be in harmony with God by being loving to the individuals around us.

Albert Schweitzer (1875-1965) was a pioneer in refocusing the attention of the theological community on the historical Jesus. In the book *Jesus at 2000*, Marcus Borg says that Schweitzer's book *Quest of the Historical Jesus* was the single most important book of New Testament scholarship in modern times. Much of his theology is focused on the command of Jesus to love God and love your neighbor as yourself. In one of his sermons Schweitzer says, "In the last analysis the command of love means this: no one is a stranger to you; every man's welfare is your concern." (Modern Religious Thought Little, Brown and company, Boston

1990 pg. 240) His life affirmed his theology. He was a very successful musician but he felt the call of God to be a medical missionary. He went to medical school and spent the rest of his life as a doctor in a hospital in Africa.

Fr. John Powell, a professor at Loyola University in the 1960's and 70's combined human potential psychology with theology. In his book Unconditional Love, he affirms that the only genuine love worthy of the name is unconditional. People struggle to love unconditionally, but we can strive for it. *Unconditional Love* is the way God loves all people. When we love we are in greater harmony with God. Jesus taught that we show love for God when we love other people. "Love demands that I learn how to focus my attention on the needs of those I love." (Unconditional Love, Argus Communications Niles, Illinois 1978 pg. 98)

Another theologian whose theology influences this view of rational Christianity was Paul Tillich (1886-1965). In his 1955 book *The New Being* (Charles Scribner's Sons, N.Y. currently out of print), he describes Christ as the new being who reveals the essence of God – the revelation of God. He is the emblem of the highest goal of man – what God wants all human beings to become. Thus, to be truly Christian is to make oneself progressively more "Christ-like" by being as loving as possible. Jesus was fully human – one of us – but his oneness with God motivated and empowered his life. This is what Jesus calls every person to be and do. Love is the essence of all existence. When we live by love, it empowers us to act justly and to work toward a just society.

This Paradigm of Rational Christianity is strongly rooted in these disciplines of Philosophy, Psychology, Theology and History. This is one way for thinking people to practice Christianity in an irrational world polluted by absolutist thinking in religion, politics and other areas of life. It is a positive way to participate in God's greatest creative experiment – the realization of a human society of peace, fulfillment and joy in the experience of LOVE.

EPILOGUE

A CHRISTIAN PSALM TO THE GOD OF LOVE

Creator God, By the Explosive power of love

You scattered the galaxy and solar systems through the vastness of space

You filled the empty space with stars and planets and moons beyond our ability to count.

Your infinite order is evident in the expanses of space and in the functioning of sub atomic structures.

The movement of stars and comets are exactly predictable.

The substructure of an atom move in consistent harmony.

> **Your unconditional love is limitless!**
> **Your compassion is unending!**

On at least one speck of stellar dust you packaged the elements and conditions for life.

You sowed the seeds for all kinds of living creatures in the sea, in the air, and on the ground.

While your material universe is clothed in perfect order

The heavenly bodies respond in precise, predictable manners.

Your world of living creatures is dynamic and progressive.

It evolves in response to changing environments and cell mutation.

Your unconditional love is limitless!
Your compassion is unending!

You endowed human beings with the creative power of the universe.

You made them free, intelligent and capable of loving.

Your highest creation is dynamically unpredictable.

They may chose to love or decide to hate.

They may join you in positive creativity

Or they may resist you in negative destructiveness.

They may seek knowledge and pursue wisdom.

Or they may celebrate ignorance and engage in folly.

Your unconditional love is limitless!
Your compassion is unending!

You have built into the moral fabric of the universe a law of reciprocity.

A universal principle that evil deeds bring negative consequences.

They sow evil deeds as the wind and they reap catastrophe as a tornado.

Your response to evil action is compassionate concern not angry outpouring of retribution.

You love all people even the most evil

But you know that their evil is ultimately self-destructive

And you care about the innocent victims of their destructiveness.

Your unconditional love is limitless!
Your compassion is unending!

Your experiment in human freedom and empowering people to love

Is in calculably hazardous and risky beyond measure.

Your goal to create a human family who live in an environment of respect, compassion, and love is consistent with your nature.

We are honored that you invite each of us to be partners in this ultimate creative adventure.

To be worthy partners we must maximize our potential for loving and minimize our propensity towards selfishness and greed.

To help us learn right living, you inspired great prophets, philosophers, saints and spiritual geniuses.

Some seers grasped part of your wisdom, but none were able to fully comprehend your love.

The ultimate revelation of your message of love came to the human family in the person of Jesus.

He was one of us, who in fully loving achieved oneness with you. His teachings, his mighty deeds of love and his humble example of service to you and for all people;

He taught us how to properly love you and how to maximize our potential for loving one another and in so doing achieve an increasing degree of oneness with you;

A world order dominated by greed, lust for power—a world where might made right, where new ideas are dangerous and love is misunderstood as weakness was not ready to hear his message.

The religious fanatics, power hungry politicians and gullible crowds determined to destroy Jesus by nailing him to a Cross and watching him die. When he was buried they thought that they had won.

Your unconditional love is limitless!
Your love is unending!

The ultimate force of Love acted to affirm forever the message of Jesus.

On the third day, You brought him back to life. He appeared to his followers to let them know that Love triumphs over Hate; Good over Evil.

You raised him to your plane and magnified the power of his Spirit so that he could become the personal spiritual guide to every person, every one who in love sought to move toward oneness with you.

To all who choose to partner with you in creations highest

adventure - creating a human family based on love, compassion and service to one another, you give eternal life.

Your unconditional love is limitless!
Your compassion is unending!

We love you and in the spirit of Jesus we enthusiastically volunteer as your partners in achieving your goal of creating a loving, creative, and compassionate human society here on Earth.

Amen! Amen!

Theological statement by Dr. George O. Elgin.